# Learning SAP S/4HANA

**An Introduction for Consultants, Beginners, and Business Users**

# Contents at a Glance

## Chapter 1: Introduction to SAP S/4HANA

- Overview of SAP S/4HANA and its evolution
- Key benefits and use cases in modern businesses

## Chapter 2: Understanding SAP ERP and S/4HANA Differences

- Comparing SAP ECC and SAP S/4HANA
- Advantages of migrating to S/4HANA

## Chapter 3: The SAP S/4HANA Architecture

- Technical architecture and key components
- On-premise vs. cloud deployments

## Chapter 4: Navigating the SAP S/4HANA User Interface

- Fiori launchpad and key navigation tips
- Personalizing the user experience

## Chapter 5: Key Functional Modules in SAP S/4HANA

- Overview of key modules: Finance (FI), Controlling (CO), Sales (SD), and more
- Core functions of each module

## Chapter 6: SAP S/4HANA Data Management

- Master data and transaction data
- Data governance and migration strategies

## Chapter 7: Getting Started with SAP S/4HANA Finance

- Introduction to the financial accounting module (FI)
- Key features of the finance module in S/4HANA

## Chapter 8: S/4HANA for Supply Chain Management

- Overview of procurement and logistics in SAP S/4HANA
- Key functionalities in Materials Management (MM) and Warehouse Management (WM)

## Chapter 9: Sales and Distribution (SD) in SAP S/4HANA

- Managing sales orders, pricing, and billing
- Overview of customer management and distribution processes

## Chapter 10: Understanding Controlling (CO) in SAP S/4HANA

- Budgeting, cost management, and financial planning
- Profitability analysis and reporting

## Chapter 11: Introduction to SAP S/4HANA Analytics

- Using embedded analytics and SAP Fiori reports
- Real-time data insights with SAP Analytics Cloud

## Chapter 12: Integrating SAP S/4HANA with Other Systems

- Integrating S/4HANA with legacy systems and third-party tools
- API management and SAP Integration Suite

## Chapter 13: Data Migration to SAP S/4HANA

- Understanding SAP's migration tools (SAP Data Services, LTMC)
- Best practices for a smooth data migration

## Chapter 14: Exploring SAP Activate Methodology

- Implementation methodology for SAP S/4HANA projects
- Phases: Discover, Prepare, Explore, Realize, and Deploy

## Chapter 15: SAP S/4HANA Cloud and On-Premise Options

- Comparing cloud and on-premise deployment models
- Choosing the right option for your organization

## Chapter 16: Best Practices for SAP S/4HANA Security

- User management and role-based access control
- Ensuring data security and compliance

## Chapter 17: Developing Custom Applications in SAP S/4HANA

- SAP Fiori app development for enhanced functionalities
- Using ABAP in the SAP S/4HANA environment

## Chapter 18: SAP S/4HANA for Business Users

- Role of business users in leveraging SAP S/4HANA functionalities
- Reporting, decision-making, and collaboration with SAP tools

## Chapter 19: Future Trends and Innovations in SAP S/4HANA

- AI, machine learning, and IoT integration in SAP S/4HANA
- The roadmap for future releases and innovations

## Chapter 20: Case Studies and Success Stories

- Real-world examples of SAP S/4HANA implementations

- Key lessons and takeaways from successful projects

This structure covers the foundational aspects of SAP S/4HANA, making it suitable for consultants, beginners, and business users alike. Let me know if you'd like to adjust or add anything!

# Chapter 1: Introduction to SAP S/4HANA

### 1.1 What is SAP S/4HANA?

SAP S/4HANA (SAP Business Suite 4 SAP HANA) is the next-generation enterprise resource planning (ERP) suite from SAP, designed to help businesses run simple in a digital world. It is built on the advanced in-memory platform SAP HANA, which enables real-time data processing and analytics for faster, smarter decision-making. SAP S/4HANA simplifies the IT landscape by streamlining data models, removing unnecessary data redundancies, and enhancing user experiences through SAP Fiori, a modern user interface technology.

Unlike its predecessor SAP ECC, which was based on traditional database technology, SAP S/4HANA leverages SAP's in-memory HANA database to perform high-speed transactions and analytics simultaneously. This new architecture allows companies to handle massive amounts of data in real time, offering a clear competitive advantage in today's fast-paced business environment.

### 1.2 Evolution of SAP S/4HANA

SAP S/4HANA represents a significant milestone in the evolution of SAP ERP systems. Prior to the launch of SAP

7

S/4HANA, SAP ERP Central Component (ECC) was the cornerstone of enterprise management for many organizations globally. However, the increasing complexity of business processes, the need for real-time insights, and the demand for digital transformation led SAP to develop a more powerful, agile system—SAP S/4HANA.

SAP ECC, which operated on various third-party databases, was efficient but not designed for the demands of the digital economy. To address this gap, SAP introduced SAP HANA in 2011, an in-memory database that dramatically enhanced data processing speed and capability. The development of SAP S/4HANA in 2015 marked the next step in integrating advanced technologies like artificial intelligence (AI), machine learning, and predictive analytics directly into the core ERP system.

### 1.3 Key Benefits of SAP S/4HANA

SAP S/4HANA is a transformative tool that offers numerous benefits to organizations seeking to stay competitive in the digital age. Below are some of the key advantages:

- **Real-time Data Processing**: Unlike traditional systems that process data in batches, SAP S/4HANA allows organizations to analyze data in real time. This instant access to insights enables faster decision-making and reduces the time to respond to market changes.

- **Simplified IT Landscape**: SAP S/4HANA consolidates data models, which simplifies the IT infrastructure. By eliminating redundant tables and aggregates, organizations can reduce data footprints and lower hardware costs.
- **Enhanced User Experience**: SAP Fiori, the user interface for SAP S/4HANA, provides a role-based, responsive, and intuitive experience. Users can access data and perform tasks easily from any device, improving productivity and user satisfaction.
- **Agility and Flexibility**: SAP S/4HANA is designed to be flexible, supporting both cloud and on-premise deployment options. It also offers easy scalability, ensuring that businesses can adapt quickly to new challenges or opportunities.
- **Advanced Analytics**: Embedded analytics in SAP S/4HANA allows users to generate reports and dashboards directly from transactional data. This integration of analytics into the core ERP system eliminates the need for separate analytical systems, saving time and resources.
- **Integration with New Technologies**: SAP S/4HANA seamlessly integrates with emerging technologies like AI, machine learning, blockchain, and the Internet of Things (IoT). These technologies enable organizations to

automate processes, predict future outcomes, and innovate faster than ever before.

## 1.4 Key Use Cases for SAP S/4HANA

SAP S/4HANA is designed for businesses of all sizes and industries, offering tailored solutions for different business sectors. Some common use cases where SAP S/4HANA provides significant value include:

- **Finance and Accounting**: SAP S/4HANA simplifies financial processes, offering real-time financial reporting, faster period-end closing, and improved cash management. Businesses can better manage liquidity, optimize financial operations, and comply with global regulations.
- **Supply Chain Management**: SAP S/4HANA enables organizations to manage their supply chains more efficiently by optimizing inventory management, procurement, and logistics operations. The system's predictive analytics capabilities help businesses forecast demand more accurately and reduce stockouts or excess inventory.
- **Manufacturing**: For manufacturing companies, SAP S/4HANA enhances production planning, asset management, and shop floor execution. By integrating IoT data with the system's analytics tools, manufacturers can achieve predictive

maintenance, reduce equipment downtime, and improve overall productivity.

- **Sales and Customer Management**: SAP S/4HANA offers powerful sales and distribution functionalities. Organizations can track the entire customer journey from order to delivery, optimize pricing strategies, and improve customer satisfaction through better service delivery.

## 1.5 The Role of SAP S/4HANA in Digital Transformation

In today's digital world, businesses are increasingly relying on technology to innovate, streamline operations, and provide better customer experiences. SAP S/4HANA plays a central role in the digital transformation journey of companies by providing them with the tools to innovate faster, adapt to new market trends, and deliver real-time insights for strategic decision-making.

One of the most critical aspects of digital transformation is the ability to break down silos across departments and functions within a business. SAP S/4HANA's integrated approach enables departments—such as finance, supply chain, and human resources—to collaborate seamlessly, ensuring that decisions are made based on unified, real-time data.

Additionally, SAP S/4HANA's integration with advanced technologies, such as AI and machine learning, allows businesses to automate routine processes, improve operational efficiency, and focus on high-value tasks like innovation and customer engagement.

**1.6 Who Should Learn SAP S/4HANA?**

SAP S/4HANA is essential for various professionals looking to grow in the digital economy. Whether you're an SAP consultant, a beginner entering the field of enterprise systems, or a business user wanting to leverage technology for better decision-making, learning SAP S/4HANA can open new career opportunities and enhance your skillset.

- **Consultants**: SAP consultants need to understand the architecture, functionality, and implementation methodologies of SAP S/4HANA to deliver successful projects for clients. Knowledge of both technical and functional aspects is critical for consultants to configure the system and align it with business needs.
- **Beginners**: Those new to ERP systems will benefit from learning SAP S/4HANA as it is one of the most advanced ERP platforms available. The skills acquired can lead to career opportunities in various roles, including ERP administration, functional consulting, and IT support.

- **Business Users**: Executives, managers, and end-users in finance, sales, logistics, and other departments can learn SAP S/4HANA to enhance their operational workflows. Business users can use the system to generate insights, streamline processes, and improve decision-making.

By the end of this chapter, readers will have a solid understanding of what SAP S/4HANA is, how it evolved, and why it is a critical tool for businesses today. This foundational knowledge will set the stage for more in-depth exploration of SAP S/4HANA's capabilities in the subsequent chapters.

In the next chapter, we will explore **Evolution from SAP ERP to SAP S/4HANA** focusing on key differences between SAP ECC and S/4HANA.

# Chapter 2: Understanding SAP ERP and S/4HANA Differences

## 2.1 Overview of SAP ERP

SAP ERP (Enterprise Resource Planning) is an integrated software solution that organizations have relied on for decades to manage business processes. First launched in the early 1990s, SAP ERP was designed to streamline operations across key areas such as finance, sales, supply chain, and human resources. It allowed companies to unify and manage data in a centralized system, improving efficiency, data accuracy, and decision-making.

For many years, SAP ECC (ERP Central Component) was the standard ERP solution offered by SAP. ECC allowed companies to store and process large volumes of data across various functions, but it relied on traditional databases. Over time, as businesses demanded more real-time insights and faster data processing, the limitations of ECC became apparent. This need for speed, agility, and innovation led to the development of SAP S/4HANA, a modern ERP solution designed for the digital age.

## 2.2 Key Differences Between SAP ERP (ECC) and SAP S/4HANA

SAP S/4HANA is not just a simple upgrade from SAP ECC; it represents a fundamental shift in how businesses use ERP systems. Below, we explore the main differences between SAP ERP and SAP S/4HANA to give you a deeper understanding of why SAP S/4HANA is the future of enterprise resource planning.

2.2.1 Database: Traditional vs. In-Memory

- **SAP ERP (ECC)**: Traditional SAP ERP runs on third-party relational databases such as Oracle, SQL Server, or IBM DB2. These databases store data on disk and retrieve it when needed, resulting in slower processing times, especially for large datasets and complex queries.
- **SAP S/4HANA**: SAP S/4HANA runs exclusively on SAP's in-memory HANA database. This means that all data is stored in memory (RAM), allowing for significantly faster data processing and real-time analytics. The in-memory architecture enables businesses to analyze massive datasets almost instantaneously, offering immediate insights for decision-making.

### 2.2.2 Data Model: Simplified Structure

- **SAP ERP (ECC)**: SAP ECC uses a traditional data model, which often involves complex and redundant data structures. For example, the system stores multiple tables for similar data points (such as totals tables and index tables), which makes reporting slower and can result in data duplication.
- **SAP S/4HANA**: One of the key innovations in SAP S/4HANA is its simplified data model. Redundant tables (such as aggregate, index, and history tables) are eliminated, reducing data footprint and storage requirements. The streamlined structure also improves processing times for both transactions and reporting. For example, the introduction of the Universal Journal (ACDOCA) in SAP S/4HANA merges financial and controlling data into a single source of truth, allowing for real-time reporting without data replication.

### 2.2.3 User Interface: SAP GUI vs. SAP Fiori

- **SAP ERP (ECC)**: The traditional SAP ECC system uses the SAP GUI (Graphical User Interface), which, while functional, is not always user-friendly. The interface can be cumbersome for new users, and it lacks the flexibility and modern design needed for today's mobile and web-based business environments.

- **SAP S/4HANA**: SAP S/4HANA introduces SAP Fiori, a modern, role-based user interface that offers a more intuitive and streamlined experience. SAP Fiori is responsive, meaning users can access it across multiple devices—desktops, tablets, and smartphones—with the same level of functionality. The interface is also customizable, allowing users to tailor the dashboard to their specific roles and preferences, enhancing productivity and ease of use.

2.2.4 Functional Enhancements and Innovations

- **SAP ERP (ECC)**: While SAP ECC is a powerful system, it has limited built-in capabilities for emerging technologies such as artificial intelligence (AI), machine learning, and predictive analytics. Integration with these technologies often requires third-party solutions or additional modules.
- **SAP S/4HANA**: SAP S/4HANA comes with built-in capabilities for advanced technologies, including AI, machine learning, predictive analytics, and the Internet of Things (IoT). These technologies allow businesses to automate processes, analyze data in real time, and make more informed decisions. For example, SAP S/4HANA's machine

learning capabilities can automate invoice
matching in accounts payable, freeing up staff
for higher-value tasks.

2.2.5 Reporting and Analytics

- **SAP ERP (ECC)**: In SAP ECC, reporting is typically
  handled through batch processing, meaning data
  is processed in predefined intervals (daily,
  weekly, etc.), and reports are generated
  afterward. This results in delayed insights, and
  users often have to rely on separate systems like
  SAP BW (Business Warehouse) for more
  advanced analytics.
- **SAP S/4HANA**: SAP S/4HANA integrates real-
  time analytics directly into the core ERP system.
  With SAP HANA's in-memory capabilities,
  businesses can run reports and analyze data as
  soon as it is entered into the system. SAP Fiori
  also provides real-time dashboards and
  visualizations, allowing users to gain insights
  from live data. This embedded analytics
  capability eliminates the need for separate
  systems, such as SAP BW, making it easier and
  faster to access critical business data.

2.2.6 Transaction Processing

- **SAP ERP (ECC)**: In traditional SAP ECC,
  transactional processes such as finance,

inventory management, and procurement are often handled in separate modules. These processes are linked, but data synchronization between them can sometimes result in delays and inefficiencies.

- **SAP S/4HANA**: SAP S/4HANA offers a more integrated approach to transaction processing. With the Universal Journal (a single source of truth for financial and controlling data), the system processes transactions and posts them in real time. This integration streamlines operations, reduces reconciliation efforts, and speeds up processes like financial close.

2.2.7 Deployment Options

- **SAP ERP (ECC)**: SAP ECC is typically deployed on-premise, meaning that organizations need to manage their own servers, storage, and IT infrastructure. While this gives companies full control, it also results in higher costs for hardware, maintenance, and upgrades.
- **SAP S/4HANA**: SAP S/4HANA offers more flexible deployment options. It can be deployed on-premise, in the cloud, or in a hybrid model (a combination of both). This flexibility allows businesses to choose the deployment model that best suits their needs, budgets, and IT strategies. Cloud deployments reduce the need

for upfront infrastructure investments and allow for faster scaling and easier updates.

2.2.8 Migration and Transition Path

- **SAP ERP (ECC)**: Migrating from SAP ECC to a newer version or another system can be complex, involving significant downtime and data migration challenges. Many organizations are still running SAP ECC but face increasing pressure to upgrade as SAP has announced it will stop supporting ECC in 2027.
- **SAP S/4HANA**: SAP has provided several migration paths for organizations moving from ECC to S/4HANA. These include greenfield (starting from scratch), brownfield (migrating existing systems), and hybrid approaches. SAP also offers tools like the SAP Readiness Check and SAP Data Migration Cockpit to help streamline the transition process and minimize disruptions to business operations.

## 2.3 Why Businesses Are Moving to SAP S/4HANA

The transition from SAP ECC to SAP S/4HANA is more than just a technical upgrade—it is a strategic move that allows businesses to thrive in the digital economy. Below are some of the main reasons why organizations are making the shift:

- **Real-Time Insights**: In today's fast-paced business environment, companies need real-time data to make informed decisions. SAP S/4HANA's in-memory computing provides instant access to insights, enabling businesses to react more quickly to market changes and customer demands.
- **Improved Efficiency**: By simplifying data models, automating processes, and reducing redundancies, SAP S/4HANA improves operational efficiency. For example, finance teams can close books faster, supply chain managers can reduce lead times, and customer service teams can resolve issues more quickly.
- **Future-Proof Technology**: SAP S/4HANA is designed with future trends in mind, including AI, machine learning, IoT, and blockchain. By moving to S/4HANA, businesses position themselves to leverage these technologies for future innovation and growth.
- **Lower Total Cost of Ownership (TCO)**: Despite the initial investment in migration, SAP S/4HANA can lead to a lower total cost of ownership over time. Cloud deployments reduce hardware costs, the streamlined data model decreases storage needs, and embedded analytics eliminate the need for separate reporting systems.

### 2.4 Conclusion: Choosing the Right ERP for the Future

While SAP ECC has served businesses well for decades, SAP S/4HANA is the future of enterprise resource planning. Its speed, agility, and advanced capabilities make it the ideal choice for organizations looking to stay competitive in the digital economy. Whether you're a business leader, consultant, or IT professional, understanding the differences between SAP ECC and SAP S/4HANA is critical for making informed decisions about the future of your ERP strategy.

This chapter has outlined the core differences between SAP ECC and SAP S/4HANA, helping you appreciate the value SAP S/4HANA brings to businesses of all sizes and industries. As you progress through the rest of this book, you'll gain a deeper understanding of how to leverage SAP S/4HANA to transform your organization and drive success in the digital age.

In the next chapter, we will explore **SAP S/4HANA Architecture** focusing on the technical structure and HANA database's unique capabilities.

# Chapter 3: The SAP S/4HANA Architecture

### 3.1 Overview of SAP S/4HANA Architecture

SAP S/4HANA is built on a sophisticated and modernized architecture designed to handle the complex requirements of today's digital businesses. The architecture revolves around the SAP HANA in-memory database, which enables real-time data processing and analytics. The entire solution is modular and highly integrated, ensuring flexibility, scalability, and efficiency across all business processes.

Understanding SAP S/4HANA architecture is key for consultants, IT professionals, and business leaders alike. It helps ensure that system implementations and customizations align with an organization's specific requirements while optimizing performance. In this chapter, we will break down the key components of SAP S/4HANA architecture and explain how they interact to deliver a streamlined, high-performance ERP system.

## 3.2 The Core Components of SAP S/4HANA

The architecture of SAP S/4HANA can be understood by examining its core components:

1. **SAP HANA Database**
2. **Application Layer**
3. **SAP Fiori User Interface**
4. **Integration with Other Systems**

3.2.1 SAP HANA Database: The In-Memory Engine

At the heart of SAP S/4HANA lies the SAP HANA database, an in-memory data platform that drives the system's unmatched speed and processing capabilities. Traditional databases store data on disk, resulting in slower data retrieval and processing times. In contrast, SAP HANA stores all data in memory (RAM), which allows it to retrieve and process data almost instantaneously.

Key characteristics of the SAP HANA database include:

- **Columnar Data Storage**: Data in SAP HANA is stored in columns rather than rows, which significantly enhances data compression and retrieval speeds. This structure is ideal for performing complex queries on large datasets.

- **In-Memory Computing**: All data is stored in RAM, allowing for faster data access, real-time analytics, and quicker transaction processing.
- **Multimodel Database**: SAP HANA supports different types of data models, including relational, graph, and document data models, enabling it to handle diverse data types.
- **Simplified Data Models**: SAP HANA simplifies data management by eliminating redundant tables (such as index tables and aggregate tables) that were essential in previous systems. This reduces data footprint and complexity, making data processing faster and more efficient.

3.2.2 Application Layer: The Digital Core

The application layer of SAP S/4HANA represents the "digital core" of the system. This layer contains the core business modules, which handle essential processes such as finance, procurement, sales, production, and supply chain management.

The key advantage of the application layer in SAP S/4HANA is its deep integration with the HANA database. The system is optimized to run directly on HANA, leveraging its real-time processing capabilities to deliver insights and execute transactions at unprecedented speeds. Unlike traditional ERP systems, which often rely on batch processing, SAP S/4HANA processes data instantly, meaning that business users can access up-to-date information at any time.

The application layer includes several functional modules, such as:

- **Finance (FI)**: Manages financial accounting, reporting, and controlling activities.
- **Sales and Distribution (SD)**: Handles customer orders, billing, and sales processes.
- **Materials Management (MM)**: Manages procurement, inventory, and logistics operations.
- **Production Planning (PP)**: Optimizes manufacturing and production activities.
- **Human Capital Management (HCM)**: Supports HR functions such as payroll, workforce management, and recruitment.

These modules interact seamlessly, offering a unified experience that simplifies operations, reduces data silos, and ensures consistency across different departments and functions.

3.2.3 SAP Fiori User Interface: The Modern User Experience

One of the standout features of SAP S/4HANA is its intuitive and role-based user interface powered by SAP Fiori. SAP Fiori transforms the way users interact with the system, offering a simple and engaging interface that is consistent across different devices, including desktops, tablets, and smartphones.

Key elements of SAP Fiori include:

- **Role-Based Design**: SAP Fiori applications are designed around specific business roles. Each user is presented with the most relevant tasks and data based on their role, ensuring that they can focus on what matters most to their job.
- **Responsive Interface**: The responsive design of SAP Fiori means that users can access the system on any device, whether they are in the office or on the go. This flexibility enhances user productivity and allows for real-time decision-making.
- **Personalization**: Users can personalize their Fiori launchpad by adding shortcuts, customizing dashboards, and arranging key tasks in a way that suits their preferences. This level of personalization improves the overall user experience and efficiency.
- **Task Automation**: Fiori applications often automate repetitive or routine tasks, reducing the time users spend on manual processes. For example, users can configure automated workflows for approvals, document generation, or status updates, reducing administrative overhead.

By combining an intuitive design with the power of SAP HANA, SAP Fiori enhances user engagement and boosts productivity.

3.2.4 Integration with Other Systems

SAP S/4HANA is not just a standalone system; it is designed to integrate seamlessly with other systems and technologies, both within and outside the SAP ecosystem. This level of integration ensures that organizations can extend the functionality of SAP S/4HANA while connecting it with third-party applications and legacy systems.

SAP S/4HANA's integration capabilities are powered by several tools:

- **SAP Cloud Platform Integration (CPI)**: This cloud-based integration service enables businesses to connect SAP S/4HANA with external systems, applications, and services. Whether integrating with legacy systems, third-party tools, or other SAP products (such as SuccessFactors or Ariba), CPI ensures smooth data exchange and process automation.
- **SAP Application Programming Interfaces (APIs)**: SAP provides a broad range of open APIs that allow businesses to extend SAP S/4HANA's functionality or integrate it with other applications. These APIs enable developers to

build custom applications or connect SAP S/4HANA with industry-specific solutions.

- **SAP Business Technology Platform (BTP)**: BTP enables the integration of new technologies such as AI, machine learning, IoT, and blockchain into SAP S/4HANA. By combining BTP with S/4HANA, businesses can automate complex processes, create predictive models, and enhance operational efficiencies with minimal effort.

## 3.3 Deployment Models: Cloud, On-Premise, and Hybrid

One of the advantages of SAP S/4HANA is its flexibility when it comes to deployment models. Businesses can choose from three primary deployment options: cloud, on-premise, or hybrid.

### 3.3.1 On-Premise Deployment

In an on-premise deployment, SAP S/4HANA is installed on the organization's servers and managed by its internal IT team. This option gives businesses full control over the system, allowing them to customize it to their specific requirements. However, on-premise deployment also requires significant infrastructure investments and ongoing maintenance, making it more expensive and resource-intensive.

### 3.3.2 Cloud Deployment

SAP S/4HANA Cloud offers a more agile, cost-effective deployment option. In the cloud model, SAP manages the infrastructure, updates, and security, allowing businesses to focus on using the system without worrying about technical maintenance. Cloud deployments are highly scalable, making them ideal for businesses looking to grow quickly or reduce their IT footprint.

- **Public Cloud**: A multi-tenant cloud environment where multiple organizations share the same infrastructure, offering lower costs and easier scalability.
- **Private Cloud**: A single-tenant cloud environment where the infrastructure is dedicated to a single organization, offering greater control and customization while maintaining the benefits of the cloud.

### 3.3.3 Hybrid Deployment

Hybrid deployment combines the best of both worlds, allowing businesses to maintain certain systems on-premise while deploying other parts of SAP S/4HANA in the cloud. This model is ideal for businesses with complex IT landscapes or those transitioning from an on-premise to a cloud environment gradually.

### 3.4 SAP S/4HANA Extensions and Customizations

SAP S/4HANA is designed to be flexible, allowing businesses to customize and extend the system to meet their specific needs. These customizations are typically built using:

- **SAP Fiori Applications**: Custom Fiori apps can be developed to enhance user experience or add new functionalities specific to a business's requirements.
- **Custom Code and Enhancements**: Businesses can develop custom code using SAP's native programming language, ABAP (Advanced Business Application Programming). SAP also offers a set of extension points to safely enhance the system without disrupting the core functionalities.
- **Embedded Machine Learning and AI**: SAP S/4HANA allows businesses to integrate machine learning models and AI algorithms into processes like invoice matching, demand forecasting, and customer service to improve accuracy and reduce manual effort.

### 3.5 The Benefits of SAP S/4HANA Architecture

The modern architecture of SAP S/4HANA provides several benefits that help organizations operate more efficiently and effectively:

- **Real-Time Processing**: SAP HANA's in-memory capabilities enable real-time transaction processing and analytics, allowing businesses to make data-driven decisions instantly.
- **Simplified IT Infrastructure**: The simplified data models reduce the complexity of managing large datasets, lowering the total cost of ownership (TCO) and improving system performance.
- **Scalability and Flexibility**: Whether deployed on-premise, in the cloud, or as a hybrid solution, SAP S/4HANA can easily scale as the business grows, offering flexibility for organizations of all sizes.
- **Enhanced User Experience**: SAP Fiori provides a consistent, intuitive, and responsive user experience across all devices, helping users perform tasks more efficiently and productively.

### 3.6 Conclusion: The Power of SAP S/4HANA Architecture

SAP S/4HANA's architecture is designed to support the modern needs of businesses, providing a platform for growth, innovation, and efficiency. With its in-memory HANA database, real-time processing, and user-friendly Fiori interface, SAP S/4HANA allows organizations to streamline operations, gain real-time insights, and stay competitive in the digital age.

As businesses continue to embrace digital transformation, the architecture of SAP S/4HANA will play a critical role in their ability to adapt, innovate, and thrive. Understanding this architecture is crucial for professionals looking to harness the full potential of SAP S/4HANA in their organizations.

# Chapter 4: Navigating the SAP S/4HANA User Interface

### 4.1 Introduction to SAP S/4HANA User Interface

One of the most significant advancements in SAP S/4HANA is the introduction of the SAP Fiori user interface, a modern, intuitive, and role-based interface that redefines how users interact with the system. SAP Fiori is designed to simplify user experience by providing a consistent, personalized, and responsive design that works across all devices—desktops, tablets, and smartphones. This shift from the traditional SAP GUI to SAP Fiori has made navigating SAP S/4HANA more user-friendly and efficient.

In this chapter, we will explore the key features of SAP Fiori, how it improves productivity, and the best practices for navigating the interface. By the end of this chapter, you will understand how to make the most of SAP Fiori's capabilities to enhance your experience with SAP S/4HANA.

### 4.2 The Evolution from SAP GUI to SAP Fiori

Historically, SAP users interacted with the system through the SAP GUI (Graphical User Interface). While functional, SAP GUI often had a steep learning curve, with a somewhat rigid design and limited flexibility. It was designed with desktop use in mind, requiring multiple steps to complete even routine tasks. As businesses moved toward mobile and cloud-based environments, SAP recognized the need for a more modern, flexible interface, leading to the development of SAP Fiori.

SAP Fiori addresses many of the limitations of SAP GUI by offering a more intuitive and responsive experience:

- **Mobile-Friendly**: SAP Fiori is optimized for all devices, allowing users to access SAP S/4HANA on their phones, tablets, or desktops with the same user experience.
- **Simplified Workflows**: Fiori applications are designed with ease of use in mind, providing users with streamlined workflows that require fewer clicks and less navigation to complete tasks.
- **Role-Based Customization**: SAP Fiori offers role-based interfaces, meaning that users see only the tools and information relevant to their job. This eliminates unnecessary complexity and improves productivity by focusing users on their key tasks.

### 4.3 Overview of SAP Fiori Launchpad

The SAP Fiori Launchpad is the entry point for users to access their Fiori apps and business applications in SAP

S/4HANA. It is designed to be a personalized, role-based workspace where users can see and access their tasks, reports, and applications with ease.

4.3.1 Key Features of the SAP Fiori Launchpad

- **Tile-Based Design**: SAP Fiori uses a tile-based layout, where each tile represents an application, task, or report. Tiles provide a visual summary, including real-time information, and are color-coded for easy identification. Each user's Launchpad displays the tiles relevant to their role, allowing for personalized access to key functions.
- **Role-Based Access**: Fiori is role-driven, meaning the layout and content of the Launchpad are tailored to the user's role within the organization. For example, a finance manager will have access to financial reporting tools, while a procurement officer will see procurement tasks and related analytics.
- **Search and Navigation**: The Launchpad includes a global search bar, enabling users to search for applications, reports, and transactions easily. Additionally, users can navigate between applications seamlessly using the breadcrumb trail and navigation menus.
- **Notifications and Alerts**: The Launchpad displays real-time notifications, such as pending approvals, overdue tasks, or system alerts. Users

can quickly respond to these notifications from within the Launchpad, ensuring that critical tasks are addressed promptly.

4.3.2 Personalizing the SAP Fiori Launchpad

SAP Fiori offers several options for personalizing the Launchpad to match a user's workflow preferences. Users can:

- **Arrange Tiles**: Drag and drop tiles to rearrange the order based on priorities.
- **Create Groups**: Organize related applications into groups, such as "Finance," "Procurement," or "HR," to keep the Launchpad organized and accessible.
- **Add or Remove Tiles**: Users can add new tiles to their Launchpad for frequently used apps or remove tiles they no longer need.
- **Set Favorites**: Mark frequently accessed applications or tasks as favorites for quicker access.

Personalization is an essential feature of Fiori, ensuring that each user can customize the system to enhance their own productivity and workflow.

## 4.4 Exploring Key SAP Fiori Applications

SAP Fiori provides a wide range of applications across different functional areas, such as finance, procurement, sales, and human resources. These applications are designed with a user-centric approach, ensuring that processes are simple and intuitive.

### 4.4.1 Finance Applications

SAP Fiori offers several finance-related apps that streamline financial operations, such as:

- **Manage Journal Entries**: This app allows finance users to create, view, and edit journal entries with real-time validation.
- **Accounts Payable Overview**: Users can monitor and manage invoices, payments, and vendors in a consolidated view, allowing for better cash flow management.
- **Cash Flow Reporting**: Finance managers can access real-time reports on cash flow, accounts receivable, and liquidity, offering instant insights into financial health.

### 4.4.2 Procurement Applications

In the procurement domain, Fiori applications help simplify purchasing and supplier management:

- **Create Purchase Orders**: This app allows users to create and manage purchase orders directly from the Fiori Launchpad, with real-time data on stock levels and vendor performance.
- **Supplier Invoices**: Users can manage supplier invoices, view payment statuses, and process payments all in one place.
- **Purchase Requisition Approval**: Procurement managers can approve purchase requisitions on the go, ensuring that the procurement process continues smoothly.

4.4.3 Sales Applications

For sales teams, SAP Fiori offers applications designed to optimize the order-to-cash process:

- **Create Sales Orders**: Sales representatives can create sales orders in real-time, with access to customer data, product inventory, and pricing details.
- **Sales Performance Dashboard**: This app provides sales managers with key metrics, such as sales volume, revenue, and customer trends, helping them make informed decisions.
- **Monitor Customer Orders**: Users can track customer orders from placement to delivery, ensuring that orders are fulfilled on time and any issues are resolved quickly.

**4.5 Working with Analytical Applications in SAP Fiori**

One of the key strengths of SAP Fiori is its ability to present real-time data in a visual format, enabling users to make data-driven decisions. Fiori analytical applications use SAP HANA's in-memory capabilities to provide users with instant access to business insights through dashboards, reports, and visualizations.

4.5.1 Overview Pages

Overview Pages are dashboards that aggregate data from multiple sources into a single view. Users can monitor critical KPIs, review performance metrics, and drill down into specific data points as needed. For example:

- **Finance Overview**: Displays key financial metrics, such as revenue, expenses, profit margins, and outstanding payments, in one place.
- **Procurement Overview**: Provides insights into purchase orders, supplier performance, and inventory levels, enabling procurement managers to make data-driven purchasing decisions.

### 4.5.2 Analytical Reports

Fiori analytical apps offer detailed reporting capabilities for different business areas. For example:

- **Sales Revenue Report**: Offers insights into sales performance by product, region, or customer.
- **Inventory Levels Report**: Allows users to track inventory status, stock movement, and replenishment needs in real-time.

### 4.5.3 Key Performance Indicators (KPIs) and Drill-Downs

Users can monitor KPIs directly from their SAP Fiori Launchpad. KPIs provide quick insights into business performance, such as:

- **Gross Margin**: A quick view of the company's profitability based on current sales and costs.
- **Order Fulfillment Rate**: Tracks the percentage of customer orders fulfilled on time.

Fiori allows users to drill down into these KPIs to explore the underlying data, identify trends, and take corrective action when needed.

## 4.6 Navigating SAP Fiori Workflows and Task Management

In addition to managing applications and analytics, SAP Fiori simplifies task management by providing a centralized view of all tasks, workflows, and approvals. Users can manage their day-to-day activities more efficiently through:

- **My Inbox App**: This app consolidates all pending tasks, such as approval requests, document reviews, and workflow activities, into a single inbox. Users can complete tasks directly from the inbox without needing to navigate to other apps.
- **Automated Workflows**: Fiori supports automated workflows, allowing routine tasks to be triggered based on predefined conditions. For example, an expense approval request can be automatically routed to the appropriate manager for review.
- **Task Delegation**: If users are unavailable, they can delegate tasks to other colleagues, ensuring that critical workflows are not delayed.

## 4.7 Best Practices for Navigating SAP Fiori

To maximize efficiency and productivity when using SAP Fiori, users should follow these best practices:

- **Use Role-Based Tiles**: Make sure that the tiles on your Launchpad are aligned with your role. Remove unnecessary tiles and focus on the tasks you perform regularly.
- **Leverage Personalization**: Personalize your Launchpad by organizing tiles, adding favorite applications, and creating custom groups for quick access.
- **Use the Search Function**: Take advantage of Fiori's global search feature to quickly find the apps, reports, or data you need without navigating through menus.
- **Stay Up to Date with Notifications**: Regularly check and act on the notifications that appear on your Launchpad to stay on top of pending tasks and alerts.
- **Explore Analytical Dashboards**: Use the built-in analytical apps and overview pages to monitor performance metrics and KPIs. Leverage these tools to make data-driven decisions in real-time.

### 4.8 Conclusion: Enhancing Productivity with SAP Fiori

Navigating SAP S/4HANA through SAP Fiori offers a powerful and intuitive user experience. The role-based, personalized interface streamlines workflows, reduces complexity, and helps users focus on what matters most in their day-to-day activities. By leveraging the tile-based Launchpad, analytical dashboards, and mobile access, businesses can enhance productivity, improve decision-making, and achieve better outcomes.

As you continue to explore SAP S/4HANA, mastering the Fiori user interface will enable you to maximize your efficiency and make the most of SAP's powerful ERP capabilities.

In the next chapter, we will explore **Key Functional Modules in SAP S/4HANA** in detail.

# Chapter 5: Key Functional Modules in SAP S/4HANA

## 5.1 Introduction to SAP S/4HANA Functional Modules

SAP S/4HANA is designed to serve as the digital core of an organization, providing an integrated suite of applications that manage every aspect of a business. These applications, or functional modules, enable companies to manage their operations, from financial transactions to supply chain logistics, production, human resources, and customer relationships. SAP S/4HANA offers both traditional ERP functionalities and new innovations that leverage its in-memory computing power.

Understanding the key functional modules in SAP S/4HANA is critical for users, consultants, and decision-makers to optimize business processes and align them with organizational goals. In this chapter, we will explore the major functional modules, their features, and how they interact to drive business success.

## 5.2 The Finance (FI) Module

The Finance (FI) module in SAP S/4HANA is one of the most essential and widely used components of the system. It is designed to manage all financial processes and transactions within an organization, including accounting, financial reporting, and statutory compliance.

## 5.2.1 Key Features of the Finance Module

- **General Ledger Accounting**: The central component of the Finance module, where all financial transactions are recorded. It integrates with other modules to provide a real-time, unified view of financial data.
- **Accounts Payable (AP)**: Manages vendor-related transactions, including invoices, payments, and vendor accounts.
- **Accounts Receivable (AR)**: Tracks customer invoices, payments, and credit management to ensure that customer balances are up to date.
- **Asset Accounting**: Manages fixed assets, including acquisitions, depreciation, and asset sales, providing a comprehensive view of asset lifecycle management.
- **Financial Closing**: SAP S/4HANA simplifies the financial closing process, allowing companies to close their books faster by automating many steps and integrating real-time financial data.

## 5.2.2 Benefits of the Finance Module

- **Real-Time Financial Reporting**: The integration with SAP HANA enables real-time financial insights and reporting, reducing delays in financial close and offering accurate financial information for decision-making.

- **Regulatory Compliance**: SAP S/4HANA provides tools to ensure compliance with various local and global financial regulations, automating reporting requirements and tax calculations.
- **Cash Management**: Organizations can manage liquidity and monitor cash flows in real time, helping finance departments make better decisions about investment and operational expenditures.

## 5.3 The Controlling (CO) Module

The Controlling (CO) module complements the Finance module by focusing on internal reporting and cost management. It enables businesses to plan, monitor, and control costs across different departments and projects, providing a detailed view of profitability and cost analysis.

5.3.1 Key Features of the Controlling Module

- **Cost Element Accounting**: Tracks and manages cost elements, such as material, labor, and overhead, and allows for cost allocation across departments and products.
- **Cost Center Accounting**: Monitors costs by organizational units, such as departments or

functions, to ensure that resources are used efficiently.

- **Internal Orders**: Allows for the tracking of costs related to specific projects or activities, enabling better control and reporting.
- **Profitability Analysis (CO-PA)**: Provides insights into the profitability of different products, customers, or market segments, helping companies optimize their offerings.

5.3.2 Benefits of the Controlling Module

- **Improved Cost Control**: With real-time data on costs and profitability, businesses can monitor performance more effectively and identify areas for cost optimization.
- **Better Decision-Making**: By providing detailed analysis of costs and profits, SAP S/4HANA's CO module supports strategic decision-making, enabling businesses to focus on the most profitable areas.

## 5.4 The Sales and Distribution (SD) Module

The Sales and Distribution (SD) module manages all activities related to sales, customer service, and distribution processes. It is critical for managing customer orders, pricing, shipping, billing, and customer relationships.

### 5.4.1 Key Features of the Sales and Distribution Module

- **Sales Order Management**: Tracks the entire lifecycle of a sales order, from the initial quotation to final delivery and invoicing.
- **Pricing and Discounts**: Manages complex pricing conditions, including discounts, taxes, and special promotions.
- **Shipping and Delivery**: Coordinates the shipping of goods to customers, including packaging, shipping schedules, and delivery confirmations.
- **Billing and Invoicing**: Automates the creation and management of invoices for products or services delivered to customers.
- **Customer Relationship Management (CRM)**: Integrates customer data, including sales history and preferences, to enhance customer interactions and improve sales performance.

### 5.4.2 Benefits of the Sales and Distribution Module

- **Faster Order Fulfillment**: SAP S/4HANA's real-time capabilities allow sales orders to be processed faster, leading to improved customer satisfaction and shorter delivery times.
- **Enhanced Customer Relationships**: By integrating customer data, sales teams can offer more personalized service, driving loyalty and repeat business.

- **Optimized Sales Operations**: The SD module provides powerful tools for sales performance analysis, enabling businesses to identify high-performing products, regions, or sales representatives.

## 5.5 The Materials Management (MM) Module

The Materials Management (MM) module manages procurement, inventory, and logistics operations, ensuring that an organization's materials are sourced and handled efficiently. It plays a central role in the supply chain by coordinating purchasing activities with inventory control and warehouse management.

### 5.5.1 Key Features of the Materials Management Module

- **Procurement**: Manages all aspects of purchasing, from requisition creation to purchase orders and supplier management.
- **Inventory Management**: Tracks the movement of materials within the organization, including stock levels, goods receipts, and goods issues.
- **Vendor Management**: Evaluates vendor performance, tracks vendor payments, and manages supplier contracts.
- **Warehouse Management**: Coordinates the storage and movement of goods in warehouses, optimizing space usage and minimizing errors.

5.5.2 Benefits of the Materials Management Module

- **Reduced Inventory Costs**: By providing real-time visibility into inventory levels and optimizing stock management, businesses can reduce carrying costs and avoid stockouts or overstocking.
- **Improved Procurement Efficiency**: The MM module streamlines procurement processes, helping companies negotiate better contracts with suppliers and automate routine purchasing tasks.
- **Optimized Supply Chain**: With end-to-end visibility into the supply chain, companies can plan better, improve logistics operations, and respond more quickly to changes in demand.

## 5.6 The Production Planning (PP) Module

The Production Planning (PP) module is crucial for manufacturing companies, as it helps manage production processes, from planning and scheduling to the actual execution of production orders.

5.6.1 Key Features of the Production Planning Module

- **Demand Planning**: Forecasts demand for products based on historical data and market trends, helping businesses optimize production schedules.

- **Material Requirements Planning (MRP)**: Ensures that the necessary materials are available for production by generating purchase requisitions and stock transfer orders.
- **Production Scheduling**: Manages the scheduling of production orders, including capacity planning and resource allocation.
- **Shop Floor Control**: Tracks production orders in real-time, ensuring that production runs efficiently and that any issues are addressed quickly.

5.6.2 Benefits of the Production Planning Module

- **Improved Production Efficiency**: By optimizing production schedules and resource usage, businesses can increase output while minimizing waste and downtime.
- **Better Demand Forecasting**: With accurate demand forecasting, companies can reduce the risk of overproduction or stockouts, aligning production with market needs.
- **Real-Time Visibility**: The PP module provides real-time insights into production progress, enabling quick adjustments to schedules or resources as needed.

**5.7 The Human Capital Management (HCM) Module**

The Human Capital Management (HCM) module helps organizations manage their workforce more effectively, from hiring and onboarding to payroll and performance management.

5.7.1 Key Features of the Human Capital Management Module

- **Employee Data Management**: Maintains comprehensive records of employee information, including personal details, job roles, and compensation.
- **Payroll**: Automates payroll processing, ensuring accurate calculations of wages, taxes, and benefits.
- **Time and Attendance**: Tracks employee work hours, leave, and absences, ensuring compliance with labor regulations.
- **Recruitment and Onboarding**: Supports the recruitment process by managing job postings, candidate screening, and onboarding.

5.7.2 Benefits of the Human Capital Management Module

- **Streamlined HR Processes**: By automating key HR functions, the HCM module reduces administrative burden and allows HR teams to focus on strategic initiatives.

- **Improved Employee Experience**: The module provides self-service capabilities for employees, allowing them to manage their own information, request leave, and view pay stubs.
- **Compliance and Accuracy**: HCM ensures that payroll, benefits, and time-tracking are accurate and compliant with local labor laws and regulations.

## 5.8 Integration Between Functional Modules

One of the greatest strengths of SAP S/4HANA is its seamless integration between functional modules. For example, a sales order processed in the Sales and Distribution (SD) module will trigger inventory checks in the Materials Management (MM) module and production planning in the Production Planning (PP) module if necessary. It will also update financial records in the Finance (FI) module.

This deep integration ensures that data flows smoothly across departments, reducing errors, eliminating redundant data entry, and providing a unified view of the business. For example:

- **Order-to-Cash Process**: When a customer places an order, the Sales module initiates processes in the Materials Management and Finance modules, streamlining order fulfillment, shipping, and billing.

- **Procure-to-Pay Process**: A purchase requisition in the Materials Management module triggers procurement, goods receipt, and payment processes, integrating the Finance module for payment and reconciliation.

## 5.9 Conclusion: Leveraging Key Functional Modules for Success

SAP S/4HANA's functional modules are the foundation of its ability to streamline and enhance business operations. By leveraging these modules, organizations can optimize their financial processes, improve supply chain efficiency, enhance customer relationships, and better manage their human resources. The real-time data and deep integration between modules empower businesses to make faster, more informed decisions and stay competitive in a rapidly changing marketplace.

In the following chapters, we will explore how to implement these modules effectively, providing practical insights for organizations looking to adopt or upgrade to SAP S/4HANA.

In the next chapter, we will explore **SAP S/4HANA Data Management** in detail.

# Chapter 6: SAP S/4HANA Data Management

## 6.1 Introduction to Data Management in SAP S/4HANA

Data management plays a crucial role in the success of any ERP system, and SAP S/4HANA is no exception. In today's data-driven world, businesses are producing vast amounts of information that need to be managed efficiently to extract value. SAP S/4HANA, with its in-memory HANA database, offers a robust platform for handling large volumes of data, ensuring that it is accessible, consistent, and accurate in real time.

In this chapter, we will explore how SAP S/4HANA manages both master and transactional data, the key tools and processes involved in maintaining data quality, and best practices for migrating and managing data within the system.

## 6.2 Types of Data in SAP S/4HANA

Understanding the types of data in SAP S/4HANA is fundamental to mastering its data management capabilities. The two main categories of data within the system are **Master Data** and **Transactional Data**.

## 6.2.1 Master Data

Master data refers to the core, static information that is essential for business processes across the enterprise. This data remains consistent over time and is shared across different functional modules. Master data typically includes:

- **Customer Data**: Information about customers, such as names, addresses, contact details, and credit limits. It is used in sales, billing, and customer service processes.
- **Vendor Data**: Data about suppliers and vendors, including contact details, payment terms, and purchasing history. Vendor data is critical for procurement and accounts payable processes.
- **Material Data**: Information about products and services offered by the company, including material descriptions, pricing, and stock levels. This data is essential for procurement, inventory management, and production processes.
- **Employee Data**: Information about employees, such as personal details, job roles, and compensation, which is used in human resources and payroll processes.
- **Financial Data**: Chart of accounts, cost centers, profit centers, and other financial data used in accounting and financial reporting.

Master data is critical because it provides the foundational information for transactions within the SAP S/4HANA system. Without accurate master data, transactional processes such as sales orders, purchase orders, and financial postings cannot occur correctly.

6.2.2 Transactional Data

Transactional data refers to the dynamic information generated through day-to-day business activities. This data is short-lived and constantly changes as new transactions are processed. Transactional data includes:

- **Sales Orders**: Generated when a customer places an order for goods or services. The sales order includes details such as the customer, products ordered, quantities, and prices.
- **Purchase Orders**: Created when a company orders goods or services from a supplier. The purchase order includes details about the vendor, the products or services being procured, quantities, and prices.
- **Financial Postings**: Transactions such as payments, invoices, and journal entries that impact financial accounts. These postings are recorded in the general ledger and other financial statements.
- **Production Orders**: Created when manufacturing activities are scheduled. These orders detail the products to be produced, the

materials required, and the planned production dates.

Both master data and transactional data must be accurately maintained to ensure that business processes run smoothly and efficiently. SAP S/4HANA provides tools and frameworks to manage these types of data effectively.

### 6.3 The Universal Journal: Simplified Data Model

One of the key innovations in SAP S/4HANA is the **Universal Journal** (ACDOCA), which consolidates financial and controlling data into a single table. In previous SAP ERP systems, financial data was spread across multiple tables, such as the general ledger, controlling tables, and material ledger tables. This setup often resulted in redundant data and slower reporting.

With the Universal Journal, all financial postings are captured in one place, eliminating the need for reconciliation between different ledgers and providing a single source of truth. This simplified data model offers several key benefits:

- **Real-Time Financial Reporting**: Because all financial data is stored in one table, SAP S/4HANA can generate financial reports in real time, without delays caused by data replication or reconciliation.

- **Simplified Data Maintenance**: The consolidation of data into the Universal Journal reduces the complexity of data maintenance, making it easier to manage and audit financial transactions.
- **Enhanced Analytics**: With all financial and controlling data in one place, organizations can perform more comprehensive and accurate analyses of their financial performance.

The Universal Journal is a powerful feature of SAP S/4HANA that streamlines financial data management and improves both operational efficiency and decision-making.

## 6.4 Data Governance in SAP S/4HANA

Data governance is essential to ensuring the quality, consistency, and security of data within SAP S/4HANA. Without proper governance, businesses can face challenges related to inaccurate data, compliance issues, and inefficient operations. SAP S/4HANA includes tools and frameworks that help enforce strong data governance practices.

6.4.1 Master Data Governance (MDG)

**SAP Master Data Governance (MDG)** is a powerful tool designed to manage the creation, maintenance, and validation of master data in SAP S/4HANA. It provides a centralized platform for managing master data across different functional areas, ensuring data quality and consistency throughout the system.

Key features of SAP MDG include:

- **Centralized Master Data Maintenance**: SAP MDG provides a single point of control for managing master data, reducing the risk of duplicate or inconsistent records.
- **Data Quality Validation**: Automated validation rules ensure that master data meets predefined quality standards before it is saved in the system. For example, customer addresses can be validated against postal code databases to ensure accuracy.
- **Approval Workflows**: SAP MDG includes workflows for the approval of master data changes, ensuring that any updates to master data are reviewed and approved by the appropriate personnel.
- **Data Synchronization**: SAP MDG ensures that master data is synchronized across all SAP systems and third-party applications, maintaining consistency across the enterprise.

6.4.2 Data Ownership and Accountability

To maintain data quality, it's important to assign clear ownership and accountability for managing data. In SAP

S/4HANA, data owners should be identified for each type of master data (such as customer, vendor, or material data). These data owners are responsible for:

- Ensuring the accuracy and completeness of the data.
- Approving changes to master data.
- Maintaining compliance with data governance policies.

By establishing clear roles and responsibilities, businesses can ensure that data is managed properly and that issues related to data quality are addressed in a timely manner.

## 6.5 Data Migration in SAP S/4HANA

For organizations implementing SAP S/4HANA, data migration is a critical step in the transition process. Migrating data from legacy systems or previous SAP versions to SAP S/4HANA requires careful planning, preparation, and execution to ensure that all data is accurately transferred.

6.5.1 SAP Data Migration Tools

SAP S/4HANA offers several tools to facilitate the data migration process, including:

- **SAP Data Services**: A comprehensive data integration and transformation tool that enables organizations to extract, transform, and load (ETL) data from various sources into SAP S/4HANA. It can handle complex data migration requirements, such as data cleansing, mapping, and validation.
- **SAP Landscape Transformation (SLT)**: A real-time replication tool that allows businesses to replicate data from SAP and non-SAP sources into SAP S/4HANA. SLT ensures that data is kept up to date during the migration process and minimizes downtime.
- **SAP S/4HANA Migration Cockpit**: A user-friendly tool specifically designed for migrating data into SAP S/4HANA. It includes predefined migration objects, such as customers, vendors, and materials, and automates many aspects of the migration process. The Migration Cockpit also includes templates for data mapping and validation, ensuring that data is migrated accurately and efficiently.

6.5.2 Data Migration Best Practices

Successful data migration requires careful planning and execution. Here are some best practices for ensuring a smooth migration to SAP S/4HANA:

- **Data Cleansing**: Before migrating data, ensure that it is accurate and complete. Remove duplicate records, correct errors, and fill in missing information to avoid issues during migration.
- **Data Mapping**: Map data from the source system to the appropriate fields in SAP S/4HANA. Ensure that all necessary data is transferred and that no important information is lost during the mapping process.
- **Testing and Validation**: Perform thorough testing to validate that data has been migrated correctly. Test the data migration process in a sandbox environment before migrating data into the live production system.
- **Incremental Migration**: If possible, migrate data incrementally rather than in one large batch. This approach reduces the risk of errors and allows for better control over the migration process.

### 6.6 Data Archiving in SAP S/4HANA

As businesses accumulate vast amounts of data over time, it is important to manage data storage effectively. SAP S/4HANA includes data archiving tools that allow businesses to archive historical data that is no longer needed for day-to-day operations but may be required for legal or regulatory purposes.

### 6.6.1 Benefits of Data Archiving

- **Optimized System Performance**: Archiving historical data reduces the size of the active database, improving system performance and reducing the load on the SAP HANA in-memory database.
- **Cost Savings**: By moving older data to cheaper storage, businesses can reduce the cost of maintaining large databases on expensive in-memory storage.
- **Regulatory Compliance**: Many industries require businesses to retain data for a specified period. Data archiving allows organizations to store this data securely while ensuring compliance with regulations.

### 6.6.2 SAP Data Archiving Tools

SAP S/4HANA provides built-in tools for managing data archiving, including:

- **Archive Development Kit (ADK)**: A framework that allows organizations to archive and retrieve data based on predefined criteria, such as transaction dates or document status.
- **Data Retention Management**: SAP S/4HANA includes tools to define data retention policies, ensuring that data is archived in accordance with legal and business requirements.

**6.7 Best Practices for SAP S/4HANA Data Management**

Effective data management is critical to ensuring the success of your SAP S/4HANA implementation. Here are some best practices to consider:

- **Establish Clear Data Governance**: Define data ownership and establish policies for managing data quality, security, and compliance.
- **Implement Master Data Management (MDM)**: Use SAP Master Data Governance (MDG) to centralize master data maintenance and ensure consistency across the organization.
- **Plan for Data Migration Early**: Begin data migration planning early in the SAP S/4HANA implementation process. Conduct data cleansing, mapping, and testing to ensure a smooth migration.
- **Leverage Real-Time Data Analytics**: Take advantage of SAP S/4HANA's real-time analytics capabilities to gain insights into business operations and make data-driven decisions.
- **Archive Data Regularly**: Implement data archiving processes to reduce the size of the active database and optimize system performance.

## 6.8 Conclusion: Unlocking the Power of Data in SAP S/4HANA

Data management is at the core of SAP S/4HANA's ability to deliver real-time insights and streamline business operations. By understanding how to manage master and transactional data, implementing strong data governance practices, and utilizing SAP's data migration and archiving tools, businesses can unlock the full potential of their data.

In the next chapter, we will explore **SAP S/4HANA's Financial Accounting (FI)** module and how it integrates with other processes to deliver real-time financial insights.

# Chapter 7: Getting Started with SAP S/4HANA Finance

## 7.1 Introduction to SAP S/4HANA Finance

SAP S/4HANA Finance is one of the core functional modules in SAP S/4HANA, designed to streamline and optimize financial management for organizations of all sizes. Built on SAP's in-memory HANA database, SAP S/4HANA Finance provides real-time financial data processing, powerful reporting, and analytics capabilities. It allows finance professionals to perform tasks such as financial accounting, management accounting, asset management, and financial close processes more efficiently.

In this chapter, we will explore the key features and components of SAP S/4HANA Finance, the benefits of real-time financial processing, and practical steps for getting started with SAP S/4HANA Finance in your organization.

## 7.2 The Components of SAP S/4HANA Finance

SAP S/4HANA Finance is a comprehensive suite of applications designed to manage all aspects of financial processes, including accounting, controlling, treasury, and risk management. It is structured around several key components:

7.2.1 Financial Accounting (FI)

The **Financial Accounting (FI)** component handles external financial reporting, ensuring that organizations comply with legal requirements and standards. It includes the following subcomponents:

- **General Ledger (GL) Accounting**: The GL is the central ledger where all financial transactions are recorded. It integrates with other functional modules to ensure that data is consistent across the organization.
- **Accounts Payable (AP)**: Manages all vendor transactions, including invoice processing, payments, and vendor reconciliation.
- **Accounts Receivable (AR)**: Tracks customer transactions, including billing, payments, and credit management.
- **Asset Accounting (AA)**: Manages the accounting for an organization's fixed assets, including acquisitions, depreciation, and disposals.
- **Financial Closing**: SAP S/4HANA Finance simplifies the period-end financial closing process by automating tasks such as accruals, reconciliations, and financial reporting.

### 7.2.2 Controlling (CO)

The **Controlling (CO)** component focuses on internal cost management and profitability analysis, providing insights into business performance. It includes:

- **Cost Element Accounting**: Tracks and categorizes costs incurred during operations, providing detailed information on cost drivers.
- **Cost Center Accounting**: Monitors costs by department or organizational unit, allowing for more precise control of expenses.
- **Internal Orders**: Enables businesses to track costs for specific projects, activities, or campaigns.
- **Profitability Analysis (CO-PA)**: Analyzes the profitability of products, customers, or market segments, helping businesses optimize their operations and improve margins.

### 7.2.3 Treasury and Risk Management

SAP S/4HANA Finance includes powerful tools for managing treasury functions and mitigating financial risks:

- **Cash Management**: Provides real-time visibility into cash flow, liquidity forecasts, and cash positions across multiple bank accounts and currencies.

- **Treasury Operations**: Manages transactions such as payments, investments, and loans, with integration to financial markets.
- **Risk Management**: Identifies and mitigates financial risks by monitoring exchange rates, interest rates, and credit exposures.

7.2.4 Financial Planning and Analysis (FP&A)

The FP&A functionality in SAP S/4HANA Finance allows organizations to plan, budget, and forecast more effectively:

- **Budget Planning**: Helps businesses allocate budgets for different departments and track actual performance against budgets.
- **Forecasting**: Provides predictive analytics tools to forecast financial performance based on historical data and market trends.
- **Financial Consolidation**: Enables companies to consolidate financial data across subsidiaries and business units for global reporting.

## 7.3 Real-Time Financial Processing with SAP S/4HANA Finance

One of the most significant advantages of SAP S/4HANA Finance is its real-time data processing capabilities, enabled by the SAP HANA in-memory database. This real-time capability offers several key benefits for financial operations:

### 7.3.1 Instant Insights into Financial Performance

Traditional ERP systems rely on batch processing, where financial data is updated at scheduled intervals. This delay can hinder decision-making, as financial reports are often based on outdated data. SAP S/4HANA Finance eliminates this problem by processing transactions in real time, providing instant insights into financial performance.

For example, finance managers can view up-to-date cash flow, accounts receivable, and profitability reports at any time, allowing for quicker responses to market changes or operational issues.

### 7.3.2 Streamlined Financial Close Process

The financial close process can be time-consuming and complex, involving multiple reconciliations, adjustments, and journal entries. SAP S/4HANA Finance simplifies this process by automating many tasks and providing a unified platform for managing financial data. This reduces the time required to close the books and ensures greater accuracy in financial reporting.

Key features that support the financial close process include:

- **Universal Journal**: The Universal Journal consolidates all financial and controlling data into a single source, eliminating the need for reconciliation between different ledgers.
- **Automated Accruals**: SAP S/4HANA Finance can automatically calculate and post accruals, reducing manual work and ensuring that expenses are recognized in the correct period.

7.3.3 Enhanced Compliance and Auditing

SAP S/4HANA Finance helps organizations comply with local and global financial regulations by providing built-in tools for managing tax, reporting, and audit requirements. The system automates tax calculations, ensures proper documentation of financial transactions, and generates regulatory reports in compliance with standards such as IFRS and GAAP.

Additionally, SAP S/4HANA Finance includes audit trails for all transactions, allowing auditors to track changes, review approvals, and verify the accuracy of financial data.

**7.4 Getting Started with SAP S/4HANA Finance**

Implementing SAP S/4HANA Finance requires a well-thought-out strategy and understanding of your organization's financial processes. Below are the key steps for getting started with SAP S/4HANA Finance.

7.4.1 Define Your Financial Processes

Before implementing SAP S/4HANA Finance, it's essential to have a clear understanding of your organization's financial processes. This includes mapping out workflows for:

- General ledger accounting
- Accounts payable and receivable
- Asset management
- Budgeting and forecasting
- Cash management
- Financial close processes

Defining these processes will help you configure SAP S/4HANA Finance to match your organization's needs and ensure that the system is set up to support your financial operations.

7.4.2 Data Migration and Integration

Data migration is a critical step in the implementation of SAP S/4HANA Finance. It involves transferring historical financial data from legacy systems into the SAP S/4HANA environment. The migration process typically includes:

- **Data Cleansing**: Ensure that financial data is accurate, complete, and free of duplicates before migrating it into SAP S/4HANA.
- **Data Mapping**: Map data fields from the legacy system to the appropriate fields in SAP S/4HANA Finance. This ensures that all necessary information is transferred correctly.
- **Testing and Validation**: Test the migrated data in a sandbox environment to ensure that it is accurate and works as expected in SAP S/4HANA Finance.

SAP provides tools like the **SAP S/4HANA Migration Cockpit** to facilitate the migration process and ensure a smooth transition.

7.4.3 Configuring the Finance Module

Once the data migration is complete, the next step is to configure SAP S/4HANA Finance based on your organization's requirements. This includes setting up:

- **Chart of Accounts**: Define the structure of your general ledger and configure accounts for different financial transactions.

- **Cost Centers and Profit Centers**: Set up cost centers and profit centers to track expenses and revenues by department, location, or business unit.
- **Tax Codes**: Configure tax codes to ensure compliance with local tax regulations.

SAP S/4HANA Finance offers flexibility in configuration, allowing you to tailor the system to meet your specific business needs.

7.4.4 User Training and Change Management

Implementing SAP S/4HANA Finance represents a significant change for your finance team, so user training is critical to the success of the system. Key areas for training include:

- Navigating the SAP Fiori user interface
- Using key financial applications (general ledger, accounts payable, accounts receivable, etc.)
- Generating financial reports and analytics
- Managing the financial close process

Change management practices should also be in place to ensure a smooth transition, including communication strategies to help employees understand the benefits of the new system and how it will improve their day-to-day work.

**7.5 Key Reports and Analytics in SAP S/4HANA Finance**

SAP S/4HANA Finance includes built-in reporting and analytics tools that provide finance professionals with real-time insights into financial performance. These tools allow users to generate reports, monitor key financial metrics, and make data-driven decisions.

7.5.1 Financial Statement Reports

SAP S/4HANA Finance includes standard reports such as:

- **Balance Sheet**: Provides a snapshot of the organization's financial position, including assets, liabilities, and equity.
- **Profit and Loss (P&L) Statement**: Tracks the company's revenues, expenses, and net income over a specified period.
- **Cash Flow Statement**: Shows the company's cash inflows and outflows, helping management monitor liquidity and cash positions.

7.5.2 Key Performance Indicators (KPIs)

SAP S/4HANA Finance provides real-time monitoring of financial KPIs, including:

- **Days Sales Outstanding (DSO)**: Measures the average time it takes to collect payment from customers.
- **Return on Investment (ROI)**: Assesses the profitability of investments made by the company.
- **Gross Margin**: Calculates the profitability of products or services before indirect costs are deducted.

7.5.3 Embedded Analytics

SAP S/4HANA Finance leverages SAP HANA's in-memory analytics capabilities to offer embedded analytics within the system. Users can create customized reports, dashboards, and visualizations without relying on external business intelligence tools. For example, finance teams can monitor real-time financial performance, compare actual results to forecasts, and analyze profitability across different business segments.

**7.6 Best Practices for SAP S/4HANA Finance**

To get the most out of SAP S/4HANA Finance, consider the following best practices:

- **Automate Routine Processes**: Leverage SAP S/4HANA Finance's automation features to streamline repetitive tasks such as journal entries, accruals, and reconciliations.

- **Utilize Real-Time Analytics**: Take advantage of the system's real-time reporting capabilities to monitor financial performance continuously and make data-driven decisions.
- **Regular Data Validation**: Ensure that financial data is accurate and up to date by implementing regular data validation and reconciliation processes.
- **Integrate Financial Data with Other Modules**: SAP S/4HANA Finance integrates seamlessly with other modules, such as sales, procurement, and production. Ensure that your financial data is linked to these processes to gain a comprehensive view of the business.

## 7.7 Conclusion: Optimizing Financial Management with SAP S/4HANA Finance

SAP S/4HANA Finance is a powerful tool that transforms how businesses manage their financial operations. Its real-time data processing, comprehensive reporting, and automation capabilities enable finance teams to work more efficiently, ensure compliance, and make better financial decisions.

As you get started with SAP S/4HANA Finance, remember to focus on defining your financial processes, ensuring accurate data migration, and training your finance team to leverage the system's full potential. By doing so, your organization can unlock new levels of efficiency and financial insight, driving success in a competitive marketplace.

In the next chapter, we will explore SAP S/4HANA's capabilities in **Supply Chain Management** and how it optimizes procurement, inventory, and logistics processes.

# Chapter 8: SAP S/4HANA for Supply Chain Management

## 8.1 Introduction to Supply Chain Management in SAP S/4HANA

Supply chain management (SCM) is a critical function for any organization that deals with the procurement, production, and distribution of goods. SAP S/4HANA provides an integrated, real-time platform for managing the entire supply chain, from procurement and inventory management to production planning and logistics. SAP S/4HANA's advanced capabilities for supply chain management allow businesses to streamline their processes, reduce costs, improve visibility, and enhance customer satisfaction.

In this chapter, we will explore how SAP S/4HANA optimizes supply chain operations by providing powerful tools for procurement, inventory management, production planning, logistics, and analytics. We will also cover how to implement and leverage these capabilities for improved efficiency and performance.

## 8.2 Key Components of Supply Chain Management in SAP S/4HANA

SAP S/4HANA's supply chain management solution is composed of several integrated modules that work together to ensure smooth and efficient supply chain operations. The core components of SCM in SAP S/4HANA include:

### 8.2.1 Materials Management (MM)

The **Materials Management (MM)** module is responsible for the procurement and inventory management processes. It ensures that the right materials are available at the right time, in the right quantities, and at the right cost.

Key functionalities of Materials Management include:

- **Procurement**: Manages all purchasing activities, from purchase requisitions to purchase orders and supplier management. This ensures timely procurement of goods and services while optimizing costs.
- **Inventory Management**: Tracks the quantity and movement of materials within an organization, including goods receipts, goods issues, and stock transfers. It provides real-time visibility into stock levels and helps prevent stockouts or overstocking.

- **Vendor Management**: Maintains relationships with suppliers, evaluates their performance, and manages contracts to ensure the organization receives the best value from its suppliers.

8.2.2 Production Planning (PP)

The **Production Planning (PP)** module focuses on planning and managing manufacturing activities. It helps companies align their production schedules with customer demand, resource availability, and material supply.

Key functionalities of Production Planning include:

- **Demand Planning**: Forecasts future demand based on historical data and market trends, helping businesses plan production schedules and procurement activities accordingly.
- **Material Requirements Planning (MRP)**: Ensures that the right materials are available for production by calculating material requirements and generating purchase requisitions or stock transfer orders.
- **Production Scheduling**: Manages the allocation of resources, such as labor and machinery, to ensure that production orders are completed on time. It also handles capacity planning to avoid bottlenecks in the production process.

- **Shop Floor Control**: Monitors the progress of production orders in real time, providing visibility into the status of manufacturing operations and ensuring that any issues are addressed quickly.

8.2.3 Warehouse Management (WM)

The **Warehouse Management (WM)** module is responsible for the efficient management of warehouse operations, ensuring that materials are stored, retrieved, and moved in a way that optimizes space and minimizes errors.

Key functionalities of Warehouse Management include:

- **Storage and Retrieval**: Manages the placement of goods in warehouses, ensuring that items are stored in optimal locations to minimize retrieval times and reduce handling costs.
- **Goods Movement**: Tracks the movement of goods within the warehouse, including inbound and outbound deliveries, stock transfers, and physical inventory counts.
- **Inventory Optimization**: Analyzes stock levels and warehouse space usage to identify opportunities for improving inventory turnover and reducing carrying costs.

8.2.4 Sales and Distribution (SD)

The **Sales and Distribution (SD)** module plays a critical role in supply chain management by managing customer orders, deliveries, and billing processes. It ensures that products are delivered to customers on time and that invoices are generated accurately.

Key functionalities of Sales and Distribution include:

- **Sales Order Processing**: Manages the entire sales order lifecycle, from order creation to delivery and invoicing. This includes checking product availability, pricing, and delivery schedules.
- **Shipping and Delivery**: Coordinates the logistics of product deliveries, ensuring that goods are shipped on time and delivered to the correct location.
- **Billing and Invoicing**: Automates the generation of invoices based on customer orders and delivery confirmations, reducing manual effort and ensuring timely billing.

8.2.5 Extended Warehouse Management (EWM)

For organizations with complex warehouse operations, **Extended Warehouse Management (EWM)** provides advanced functionality to manage larger and more intricate warehouses. EWM offers more granular control over warehouse processes, such as:

- **Optimized Picking and Packing**: EWM supports efficient picking and packing strategies, ensuring that orders are fulfilled quickly and accurately.
- **Resource Management**: Tracks the utilization of warehouse resources, such as forklifts and personnel, to optimize workflow and reduce idle time.
- **Yard Management**: Manages the movement of trucks and trailers within the warehouse yard, ensuring smooth inbound and outbound logistics.

8.2.6 Transportation Management (TM)

The **Transportation Management (TM)** module manages the transportation of goods from suppliers to warehouses and from warehouses to customers. TM ensures that shipments are planned, executed, and tracked efficiently, minimizing transportation costs while meeting delivery timelines.

Key functionalities of Transportation Management include:

- **Shipment Planning**: Optimizes transportation routes and carrier selection to minimize costs and ensure timely delivery of goods.

- **Freight Cost Management**: Tracks transportation costs and manages freight agreements to ensure that shipping expenses are kept under control.
- **Shipment Tracking**: Provides real-time visibility into the status of shipments, helping businesses monitor delivery progress and address any delays or issues.

## 8.3 Real-Time Supply Chain Visibility with SAP S/4HANA

One of the key advantages of SAP S/4HANA is its ability to provide real-time visibility into all aspects of the supply chain. By leveraging the in-memory SAP HANA database, businesses can access up-to-the-minute information on inventory levels, production progress, order statuses, and transportation movements.

8.3.1 Real-Time Inventory Management

With SAP S/4HANA's real-time inventory management capabilities, businesses can monitor stock levels across multiple locations and warehouses. This visibility allows for better decision-making, ensuring that inventory levels are optimized to meet customer demand while avoiding excess stock.

Key benefits of real-time inventory management include:

- **Reduced Stockouts**: Real-time tracking of stock levels helps businesses avoid stockouts by triggering automatic reorder points and purchase requisitions.
- **Optimized Replenishment**: SAP S/4HANA's material requirements planning (MRP) functionality ensures that inventory is replenished based on actual demand, reducing the need for excess inventory and lowering carrying costs.

8.3.2 End-to-End Production Visibility

In the production environment, SAP S/4HANA provides real-time insights into the status of production orders, resource availability, and shop floor activities. This visibility enables production managers to monitor manufacturing processes closely, ensuring that production schedules are met and that any issues are addressed before they impact delivery timelines.

Key benefits of real-time production visibility include:

- **Proactive Issue Resolution**: By identifying potential bottlenecks or resource shortages in real time, production teams can take corrective action to prevent delays.

- **Improved Resource Utilization**: SAP S/4HANA provides insights into machine and labor capacity, allowing production managers to allocate resources more effectively and reduce downtime.

8.3.3 Real-Time Logistics and Transportation Tracking

SAP S/4HANA integrates transportation management with warehouse and sales processes, providing real-time tracking of shipments from the moment goods leave the warehouse to their delivery at the customer's location. This real-time visibility helps businesses monitor transportation performance and manage logistics more effectively.

Key benefits of real-time logistics tracking include:

- **On-Time Deliveries**: By tracking the status of shipments in real time, businesses can ensure that deliveries are made on time and that any delays are communicated to customers proactively.
- **Reduced Transportation Costs**: Real-time visibility into transportation routes and carrier performance allows businesses to optimize shipping strategies and reduce costs.

### 8.4 Integration of Supply Chain Processes in SAP S/4HANA

One of the most significant advantages of using SAP S/4HANA for supply chain management is the seamless integration of all supply chain processes, from procurement and production to distribution and customer service. This integration eliminates data silos and ensures that all departments work with the same real-time information.

8.4.1 Procurement to Pay Process

In SAP S/4HANA, the procurement to pay process is fully integrated, ensuring that procurement, inventory, and accounts payable departments have access to consistent data. When a purchase order is created, it automatically triggers updates in inventory and financial accounting, ensuring that stock levels are adjusted, and invoices are processed accurately.

8.4.2 Order to Cash Process

The order to cash process in SAP S/4HANA ensures that customer orders are processed efficiently from start to finish. When a sales order is created, the system checks product availability, schedules deliveries, and generates invoices. This end-to-end integration ensures that sales, logistics, and finance teams work in harmony to fulfill customer orders on time and manage receivables effectively.

8.4.3 Plan to Produce Process

The plan to produce process integrates demand planning, material requirements planning, and production scheduling. This integration ensures that production is aligned with customer demand and that the necessary materials are available to complete production orders on time.

## 8.5 Analytics and Reporting in SAP S/4HANA Supply Chain Management

SAP S/4HANA's embedded analytics capabilities provide powerful tools for analyzing supply chain performance and identifying areas for improvement. By leveraging real-time data from across the supply chain, businesses can generate actionable insights that drive better decision-making.

8.5.1 Key Performance Indicators (KPIs)

SAP S/4HANA allows businesses to track key supply chain KPIs in real time, including:

- **Order Fulfillment Rate**: Measures the percentage of customer orders fulfilled on time and in full.

- **Inventory Turnover**: Tracks how efficiently inventory is being used by measuring the number of times inventory is sold and replaced over a given period.
- **Lead Time**: Monitors the time it takes to fulfill a customer order, from order placement to delivery.

### 8.5.2 Real-Time Dashboards and Reports

SAP S/4HANA's embedded analytics provide real-time dashboards and reports that allow supply chain managers to monitor performance across all areas of the supply chain. These dashboards can be customized to display the most relevant data for each role, helping managers focus on the metrics that matter most to their operations.

### 8.5.3 Predictive Analytics and Forecasting

SAP S/4HANA includes predictive analytics tools that allow businesses to forecast future demand, production schedules, and inventory needs based on historical data and market trends. These tools help businesses anticipate changes in demand and adjust their supply chain strategies accordingly.

**8.6 Best Practices for Implementing SAP S/4HANA Supply Chain Management**

To get the most out of SAP S/4HANA's supply chain management capabilities, consider the following best practices:

- **Leverage Real-Time Data**: Use SAP S/4HANA's real-time data processing capabilities to monitor inventory levels, production progress, and shipment statuses continuously. Real-time visibility allows for faster decision-making and reduces the risk of delays or stockouts.
- **Optimize Inventory Management**: Implement best practices for inventory management, such as setting accurate reorder points and using MRP to automate procurement processes. This will help minimize excess inventory and reduce carrying costs.
- **Integrate Supply Chain Processes**: Ensure that procurement, production, logistics, and finance processes are fully integrated within SAP S/4HANA to improve coordination and reduce errors.
- **Monitor Supply Chain KPIs**: Regularly track and analyze key supply chain performance indicators to identify areas for improvement and optimize operations.

### 8.7 Conclusion: Enhancing Supply Chain Efficiency with SAP S/4HANA

SAP S/4HANA offers a comprehensive, real-time solution for managing supply chain operations. By integrating procurement, production, inventory, logistics, and distribution processes, SAP S/4HANA enables businesses to operate more efficiently and respond quickly to changes in customer demand and market conditions.

In this chapter, we've explored the key components of SAP S/4HANA's supply chain management capabilities, how they are integrated, and the benefits of real-time visibility and analytics. By leveraging SAP S/4HANA's powerful tools for supply chain management, organizations can reduce costs, improve operational efficiency, and deliver better service to their customers.

In the next chapter, we will explore **Sales and Distribution (SD) in SAP S/4HANA**.

# Chapter 9: Sales and Distribution (SD) in SAP S/4HANA

### 9.1 Introduction to Sales and Distribution (SD) in SAP S/4HANA

The **Sales and Distribution (SD)** module in SAP S/4HANA plays a central role in managing an organization's end-to-end sales processes, from handling customer inquiries and sales orders to shipping products and managing billing and invoicing. The SD module is designed to ensure that businesses can streamline their sales operations, improve customer satisfaction, and maximize revenue.

By integrating with other functional modules such as **Materials Management (MM)**, **Production Planning (PP)**, and **Finance (FI)**, SAP S/4HANA's SD module helps organizations manage the entire sales lifecycle, from product availability checks to revenue recognition. This chapter will explore the key features of the SD module, how it interacts with other modules, and how to get started with configuring and using SD in your organization.

## 9.2 Key Components of the Sales and Distribution Module

SAP S/4HANA's Sales and Distribution module is composed of several sub-modules and functionalities that cover different aspects of the sales process. These components work together to manage sales orders, pricing, deliveries, and billing.

### 9.2.1 Sales Order Management

Sales order management is at the heart of the SD module. It enables companies to create, manage, and track customer orders from initial inquiry to order fulfillment and invoicing.

Key functionalities include:

- **Sales Order Creation**: The system allows users to create sales orders by entering customer data, products, quantities, and delivery schedules. Sales orders can be generated manually or automatically based on customer inquiries, quotations, or contracts.
- **Availability Check**: During sales order creation, SAP S/4HANA performs an availability check to ensure that the requested products are available in stock or can be produced in time to meet the customer's delivery requirements.

- **Order Confirmation**: Once a sales order is created, the system automatically generates an order confirmation, which is sent to the customer to confirm the details of the order, including prices, delivery dates, and shipping information.

9.2.2 Pricing and Discounts

Pricing in SAP S/4HANA SD is highly flexible and configurable, allowing businesses to manage complex pricing conditions and discount structures for different customers and products.

Key features of the pricing functionality include:

- **Condition Types**: SAP S/4HANA uses condition types to determine pricing factors such as product price, discounts, surcharges, taxes, and freight. These condition types are applied based on predefined rules and customer-specific agreements.
- **Price Lists**: Businesses can maintain different price lists for various customer segments or regions. The system automatically selects the appropriate price list based on the customer and sales order conditions.
- **Discounts and Promotions**: SAP S/4HANA SD allows users to apply discounts, rebates, and promotions to sales orders based on predefined

criteria. For example, volume discounts can be offered when customers purchase large quantities, or seasonal promotions can be applied automatically.

9.2.3 Shipping and Delivery

The shipping and delivery process in SAP S/4HANA SD ensures that products are delivered to customers on time and in the right condition. This process involves the coordination of logistics activities such as packing, shipping, and tracking deliveries.

Key functionalities include:

- **Delivery Creation**: Once a sales order is confirmed, the system automatically generates a delivery document, specifying the products to be shipped, quantities, and shipping details. Deliveries can be managed for individual orders or consolidated for multiple orders.
- **Picking and Packing**: SAP S/4HANA supports the picking and packing of products in the warehouse. Users can create picking lists and packing instructions, ensuring that products are prepared for shipment efficiently.
- **Shipping and Freight Management**: The system integrates with transportation management to optimize shipping routes, select carriers, and calculate freight costs. Shipping documents such

as waybills and packing slips are generated automatically.

- **Delivery Tracking**: SAP S/4HANA allows businesses to track the status of deliveries in real time, ensuring that any delays or issues are addressed promptly.

9.2.4 Billing and Invoicing

Billing and invoicing are critical to ensuring that businesses collect revenue in a timely manner. SAP S/4HANA SD automates the billing process, generating accurate invoices based on sales orders and deliveries.

Key functionalities include:

- **Invoice Creation**: The system automatically generates invoices once goods have been delivered. Invoices are based on the delivery and pricing information from the sales order, ensuring that customers are billed accurately.
- **Billing Types**: SAP S/4HANA supports different types of billing, including standard billing, collective billing (where multiple deliveries are consolidated into a single invoice), and periodic billing (for subscription or recurring services).
- **Credit Management**: The system integrates with SAP's credit management functionality to ensure that customers' credit limits are monitored and enforced. In case of overdue payments or

exceeded credit limits, the system can block further sales orders or deliveries.
- **Revenue Recognition**: SAP S/4HANA includes revenue recognition tools that ensure revenue is recognized according to accounting standards, whether based on delivery, completion of services, or other criteria.

9.2.5 Customer Relationship Management (CRM) Integration

SAP S/4HANA SD integrates with SAP's Customer Relationship Management (CRM) solution to enhance the customer experience by providing a 360-degree view of customer interactions, preferences, and history.

Key features of CRM integration include:

- **Customer Data Management**: SAP S/4HANA allows businesses to maintain comprehensive customer profiles, including contact details, purchasing history, preferences, and communication preferences.
- **Sales Campaigns and Marketing**: Businesses can create targeted sales campaigns and marketing promotions based on customer data, helping to improve customer engagement and drive sales.
- **Customer Support and Service**: SAP S/4HANA integrates with customer service functions,

allowing businesses to manage service requests, complaints, and returns efficiently.

## 9.3 Integration of SD with Other SAP Modules

One of the key strengths of SAP S/4HANA is its seamless integration between different modules, ensuring that data flows smoothly across the organization. The SD module is tightly integrated with other key modules such as Materials Management (MM), Production Planning (PP), and Finance (FI), ensuring that sales, inventory, production, and financial data are always up to date.

### 9.3.1 Integration with Materials Management (MM)

The SD module is integrated with the **Materials Management (MM)** module to ensure that product availability is checked in real time during sales order creation. When a sales order is placed, the system checks whether the products are available in stock or whether they need to be procured or produced.

If products need to be procured, the system can trigger purchase requisitions in the MM module. This ensures that inventory levels are always aligned with customer demand and that stockouts are minimized.

### 9.3.2 Integration with Production Planning (PP)

For companies that manufacture products, the SD module integrates with the **Production Planning (PP)** module to ensure that production schedules are aligned with customer orders. When a sales order for a manufactured product is created, the system can trigger production orders in the PP module, ensuring that the products are produced in time for delivery.

This integration helps businesses optimize production schedules and minimize lead times, ensuring that customer orders are fulfilled on time.

### 9.3.3 Integration with Finance (FI)

The **Finance (FI)** module is closely integrated with SD to ensure that financial transactions related to sales are recorded accurately. When an invoice is generated in SD, the system automatically posts the revenue and accounts receivable entries in the general ledger. Similarly, any credit memos, discounts, or rebates are reflected in the financial accounts.

This integration ensures that the company's financial statements are always up to date, providing an accurate view of revenue, accounts receivable, and cash flow.

## 9.4 Key Reports and Analytics in SAP S/4HANA SD

SAP S/4HANA includes built-in analytics and reporting tools that provide real-time insights into sales performance, customer behavior, and order fulfillment. These tools enable businesses to make data-driven decisions and optimize their sales operations.

9.4.1 Sales Performance Reports

SAP S/4HANA SD provides a variety of sales performance reports that track key metrics such as:

- **Sales Revenue**: Measures total sales revenue over a specific period, broken down by product, region, or customer segment.
- **Sales Order Fulfillment**: Tracks the percentage of customer orders fulfilled on time and in full, providing insights into delivery performance and customer satisfaction.
- **Top Customers and Products**: Identifies the top customers and products in terms of revenue, helping businesses focus on their most valuable relationships and product lines.

9.4.2 Customer Analytics

Customer analytics in SAP S/4HANA SD helps businesses understand customer behavior and preferences. Key reports include:

103

- **Customer Lifetime Value**: Measures the total value of a customer over their lifetime with the business, helping sales teams prioritize high-value customers.
- **Customer Churn**: Tracks customer churn rates and identifies at-risk customers, allowing businesses to take proactive steps to retain customers.
- **Sales Conversion Rates**: Analyzes the conversion rates from customer inquiries and quotations to actual sales orders, helping businesses identify opportunities to improve their sales process.

9.4.3 Order Management Reports

SAP S/4HANA SD provides real-time visibility into order statuses and fulfillment rates. Key reports include:

- **Order Backlogs**: Tracks orders that have not yet been fulfilled, providing insights into potential bottlenecks in the order fulfillment process.
- **Order Cycle Times**: Measures the time it takes to process and fulfill sales orders, helping businesses identify opportunities to streamline their order-to-cash process.
- **Invoice Aging**: Monitors outstanding invoices and payment due dates, helping finance teams manage accounts receivable and improve cash flow.

### 9.5 Best Practices for SAP S/4HANA SD Implementation

To ensure the successful implementation and use of SAP S/4HANA's Sales and Distribution module, businesses should follow these best practices:

9.5.1 Define Clear Sales Processes

Before implementing SAP S/4HANA SD, it is essential to clearly define your sales processes, including how sales orders are created, how pricing is managed, and how deliveries and billing are handled. This will ensure that the system is configured to meet your specific business needs.

9.5.2 Leverage Real-Time Analytics

Use SAP S/4HANA's real-time analytics capabilities to monitor sales performance continuously. By tracking sales revenue, order fulfillment, and customer satisfaction metrics, businesses can make informed decisions to optimize sales strategies and improve customer service.

9.5.3 Integrate with Other Modules

Ensure that your SD module is fully integrated with other SAP modules, such as MM, PP, and FI. This integration will enable seamless data flow across the organization, ensuring that inventory, production, and financial data are always up to date.

### 9.5.4 Automate Pricing and Discounts

Leverage SAP S/4HANA's pricing engine to automate complex pricing and discount structures. This will reduce manual effort and ensure that customers are billed accurately and consistently.

### 9.5.5 Regularly Update Customer and Sales Data

Maintain accurate and up-to-date customer and sales data in SAP S/4HANA to ensure that the system can generate reliable reports and insights. Regularly review and clean up customer profiles, sales orders, and pricing data to avoid inconsistencies.

## 9.6 Conclusion: Driving Sales Success with SAP S/4HANA SD

The Sales and Distribution module in SAP S/4HANA is a powerful tool for managing the end-to-end sales process, from customer inquiries and orders to deliveries and invoicing. By leveraging the real-time capabilities of SAP S/4HANA, businesses can streamline their sales operations, improve customer satisfaction, and drive revenue growth.

In this chapter, we've covered the key components of SAP S/4HANA SD, including sales order management, pricing, shipping, billing, and customer analytics. By implementing best practices and integrating SD with other functional modules, businesses can optimize their sales processes and gain a competitive edge in the marketplace.

In the next chapter, we will explore **Controlling (CO) in SAP S/4HANA** in detail.

# Chapter 10: Understanding Controlling (CO) in SAP S/4HANA

## 10.1 Introduction to the Controlling (CO) Module in SAP S/4HANA

The **Controlling (CO)** module in SAP S/4HANA is a key component for managing internal financial performance and controlling costs. It provides organizations with the tools to track, plan, analyze, and report costs and revenues. The CO module complements the **Financial Accounting (FI)** module by focusing on internal management accounting, enabling businesses to monitor profitability and efficiency across departments, products, projects, and processes.

SAP S/4HANA's CO module integrates seamlessly with other functional areas such as **Production Planning (PP)**, **Materials Management (MM)**, and **Sales and Distribution (SD)**, ensuring that data flows smoothly and that costs are accurately allocated. In this chapter, we will explore the key components of the Controlling module, its functionality, and how it supports decision-making in areas like cost control, profitability analysis, and internal reporting.

## 10.2 Key Components of the Controlling (CO) Module

The SAP S/4HANA CO module consists of several subcomponents that provide a comprehensive framework for managing internal costs and profitability. The main components of CO include:

10.2.1 Cost Element Accounting (CEA)

**Cost Element Accounting** tracks the sources of costs and revenues within an organization. It is essential for categorizing and analyzing expenses and income, allowing businesses to differentiate between direct costs (such as raw materials and labor) and indirect costs (such as overheads).

Key functionalities include:

- **Primary Cost Elements**: These represent direct costs and revenues that originate outside the organization, such as material costs, payroll expenses, and sales revenue. Primary cost elements correspond to general ledger accounts in the Financial Accounting (FI) module.
- **Secondary Cost Elements**: These represent internal costs incurred within the organization, such as production overheads or internal service allocations. Secondary cost elements are used exclusively in the CO module for internal reporting and cost allocation.

Cost Element Accounting provides a detailed breakdown of where costs are incurred and helps managers identify opportunities for cost optimization.

10.2.2 Cost Center Accounting (CCA)

**Cost Center Accounting** is a tool for monitoring and controlling costs by organizational units or departments. A cost center represents an area of the business where costs are incurred, such as a production department, sales office, or administrative unit. Cost centers are used to track operational expenses and analyze how resources are being utilized.

Key functionalities include:

- **Cost Center Hierarchies**: Businesses can create hierarchies of cost centers to organize departments or functional areas logically. For example, a manufacturing company might have separate cost centers for each production line, with a parent cost center for the entire production department.
- **Cost Allocations**: Cost Center Accounting supports cost allocations, where costs from one cost center (such as utilities or IT support) are distributed to other cost centers based on usage or predefined rules. This ensures that costs are accurately assigned to the departments that benefit from the services.

- **Cost Variance Analysis**: Managers can analyze variances between planned and actual costs at the cost center level, helping identify inefficiencies and opportunities for cost savings.

10.2.3 Internal Orders

**Internal Orders** are temporary cost objects used to track specific activities, projects, or campaigns within the organization. They are commonly used for short-term projects, such as marketing campaigns, R&D initiatives, or event planning. Internal orders provide detailed tracking of costs and allow businesses to monitor the profitability of specific initiatives.

Key functionalities include:

- **Order Types**: Businesses can define different types of internal orders based on their purpose, such as investment orders (for capital projects), overhead orders (for tracking indirect costs), or revenue-generating orders (for service projects).
- **Budgeting and Cost Monitoring**: Internal Orders support budgeting functionality, allowing managers to set cost limits for projects and monitor spending against the budget in real time.
- **Settlement of Costs**: Once an internal order is completed, costs can be settled (transferred) to other cost objects such as cost centers,

profitability segments, or assets. This ensures that the final costs are reflected in the appropriate financial statements.

10.2.4 Activity-Based Costing (ABC)

**Activity-Based Costing (ABC)** is a method of assigning overhead costs to products, services, or customers based on their consumption of activities. This approach provides a more accurate representation of cost drivers and helps businesses understand the true cost of producing goods or delivering services.

Key functionalities include:

- **Activity Types**: Businesses can define different activity types, such as machine hours, labor hours, or IT services, which represent the resources consumed by a cost center.
- **Cost Allocation Based on Activities**: Costs are allocated based on the number of activity units consumed by each product, service, or department. For example, if a product requires 10 hours of machine time, the associated overhead costs are allocated accordingly.
- **Improved Cost Accuracy**: ABC provides greater accuracy in cost allocation by identifying specific activities that drive costs, helping businesses identify inefficiencies and areas for improvement.

10.2.5 Profit Center Accounting (PCA)

**Profit Center Accounting (PCA)** enables businesses to evaluate the profitability of different parts of the organization. A profit center represents a unit of the organization responsible for generating revenue and managing its own costs, such as a product line, geographical region, or business unit.

Key functionalities include:

- **Profit Center Hierarchies**: Businesses can create hierarchical structures of profit centers to represent their organizational model. This allows for profitability reporting at different levels, such as individual product lines, regions, or the entire organization.
- **Internal Profitability Analysis**: Profit Center Accounting allows managers to analyze internal profitability by comparing revenues and expenses at the profit center level. This helps identify the most profitable parts of the business and areas that need improvement.
- **Performance Measurement**: Businesses can use PCA to measure the financial performance of different business units, enabling better resource allocation and strategic decision-making.

10.2.6 Profitability Analysis (CO-PA)

**Profitability Analysis (CO-PA)** is one of the most powerful tools in the CO module, allowing businesses to analyze profitability by various dimensions, such as product, customer, region, or sales channel. CO-PA provides detailed insights into the drivers of revenue and costs, helping businesses optimize their operations and improve margins.

There are two types of profitability analysis in SAP S/4HANA:

- **Costing-Based CO-PA**: Tracks costs and revenues using cost elements. It provides real-time profitability reporting and is useful for organizations that need immediate insights into their profit margins.
- **Account-Based CO-PA**: Tracks profitability based on general ledger accounts. This method ensures that the profitability data is fully reconciled with the financial accounting data, providing more accurate financial reporting.

Key functionalities include:

- **Revenue and Cost Analysis by Segment**: CO-PA allows businesses to analyze profitability at a granular level, such as by customer, product line, or geographical region. This helps identify high-margin products or profitable customers, as well as areas where costs can be reduced.

- **Contribution Margin Analysis**: CO-PA supports the calculation of contribution margins, which measure the profitability of products or business segments before deducting fixed costs.
- **Predictive Analytics and Forecasting**: With SAP S/4HANA's real-time analytics capabilities, CO-PA enables businesses to forecast future profitability based on historical data, market trends, and sales forecasts.

**10.3 Integration of CO with Other SAP Modules**

The Controlling (CO) module is fully integrated with other SAP S/4HANA modules, ensuring that costs and revenues are accurately captured and allocated throughout the organization. The most significant integrations include:

10.3.1 Integration with Financial Accounting (FI)

The integration between **Controlling (CO)** and **Financial Accounting (FI)** ensures that all financial transactions are aligned and recorded correctly in both internal and external reporting. For example:

- Costs incurred in CO (such as production costs) are posted to the appropriate general ledger accounts in FI.

- Revenues recorded in FI are automatically reflected in CO-PA for profitability analysis.

This integration ensures that internal management accounting (CO) and external financial accounting (FI) are fully aligned, providing consistent financial data across the organization.

10.3.2 Integration with Production Planning (PP)

The CO module is integrated with **Production Planning (PP)** to ensure that production costs are accurately captured and allocated to the appropriate cost centers or internal orders. For example:

- Direct production costs, such as raw materials and labor, are posted to the relevant cost centers in CO.
- Overhead costs, such as machine maintenance or utilities, are allocated to production orders based on activity consumption.

This integration provides real-time visibility into production costs and helps businesses manage their manufacturing operations more effectively.

10.3.3 Integration with Sales and Distribution (SD)

The integration between **Sales and Distribution (SD)** and CO ensures that sales revenues and costs are tracked in real time, enabling profitability analysis and cost allocation:

- Sales orders generated in SD trigger cost allocations in CO, such as sales commissions or delivery costs.
- Revenues from customer invoices are posted to CO-PA, allowing businesses to analyze profitability by customer, product, or region.

This integration provides a complete picture of sales performance and profitability, helping businesses optimize their pricing strategies and customer relationships.

10.3.4 Integration with Materials Management (MM)

The **Materials Management (MM)** module is integrated with CO to ensure that material costs are accurately tracked and allocated. For example:

- When materials are procured, the associated costs are posted to cost centers or internal orders in CO.
- When materials are issued for production, the costs are allocated to production orders, ensuring that material consumption is accurately reflected in production costs.

This integration helps businesses manage their procurement and inventory processes more efficiently, reducing waste and optimizing resource allocation.

## 10.4 Real-Time Reporting and Analytics in SAP S/4HANA CO

One of the key advantages of SAP S/4HANA's CO module is its ability to provide real-time insights into costs, revenues, and profitability. SAP S/4HANA leverages the in-memory HANA database to enable real-time reporting and analytics, allowing businesses to make data-driven decisions more quickly.

10.4.1 Cost Center Reports

Cost center reports in SAP S/4HANA CO provide detailed insights into the costs incurred by different departments or organizational units. These reports allow managers to:

- Analyze variances between planned and actual costs.
- Identify cost drivers and inefficiencies in specific cost centers.
- Monitor cost allocations and ensure that shared costs are distributed appropriately.

## 10.4.2 Profitability Reports

Profitability reports generated through CO-PA provide insights into the profitability of products, customers, regions, and sales channels. These reports help businesses:

- Identify the most profitable products and customers.
- Analyze contribution margins by segment.
- Forecast future profitability based on historical data and market trends.

## 10.4.3 Real-Time Dashboards and KPIs

SAP S/4HANA CO includes real-time dashboards that display key performance indicators (KPIs) related to costs and profitability. These dashboards provide a visual representation of financial performance, allowing managers to monitor cost efficiency, resource utilization, and profitability in real time.

## 10.5 Best Practices for Implementing SAP S/4HANA CO

To ensure the successful implementation of the Controlling (CO) module, businesses should follow these best practices:

### 10.5.1 Define Clear Cost Structures

Before implementing SAP S/4HANA CO, businesses should define clear cost structures, including cost centers, profit centers, and internal orders. This will ensure that costs are accurately tracked and allocated to the appropriate parts of the organization.

### 10.5.2 Automate Cost Allocations

Leverage SAP S/4HANA's automation capabilities to streamline cost allocations. For example, use predefined allocation rules to automatically distribute overhead costs across departments based on activity consumption or usage.

### 10.5.3 Monitor Profitability Regularly

Regularly monitor profitability using CO-PA reports and dashboards. Analyze contribution margins by product, customer, or region to identify areas for improvement and optimize pricing strategies.

### 10.5.4 Integrate CO with Other Modules

Ensure that the CO module is fully integrated with other SAP S/4HANA modules, such as FI, PP, SD, and MM. This integration will provide a complete view of costs and revenues across the organization and ensure that financial data is consistent and accurate.

## 10.6 Conclusion: Optimizing Cost Control and Profitability with SAP S/4HANA CO

The Controlling (CO) module in SAP S/4HANA is a powerful tool for managing internal costs, profitability, and resource allocation. By leveraging the real-time capabilities of SAP S/4HANA, businesses can gain greater visibility into their financial performance, optimize costs, and improve profitability.

In this chapter, we explored the key components of the CO module, including cost element accounting, cost center accounting, internal orders, and profitability analysis. By following best practices and integrating CO with other functional modules, businesses can drive financial efficiency and make data-driven decisions that enhance their overall performance.

In the next chapter, we will explore **SAP S/4HANA Analytics**.

# Chapter 11: Introduction to SAP S/4HANA Analytics

## 11.1 Introduction to Analytics in SAP S/4HANA

In today's fast-paced, data-driven business environment, having real-time access to data and actionable insights is critical for making informed decisions. SAP S/4HANA offers built-in **analytics capabilities** that enable businesses to perform advanced reporting, monitor key performance indicators (KPIs), and gain deeper insights into their operations. These analytics tools, powered by the **SAP HANA in-memory database**, provide organizations with the ability to analyze large volumes of data in real time, driving improved decision-making and operational efficiency.

SAP S/4HANA's embedded analytics transforms the traditional approach to business intelligence (BI) by integrating analytics directly into transactional processes. This integration enables users to generate reports and dashboards within the core system without needing separate data warehouses or BI platforms. In this chapter, we will explore the key features of SAP S/4HANA analytics, its architecture, and how businesses can use these tools to gain real-time insights and optimize their operations.

### 11.2 SAP S/4HANA Analytics Architecture

SAP S/4HANA's analytics capabilities are built on a modern architecture that leverages the in-memory **SAP HANA** platform for high-speed data processing. This architecture enables businesses to run analytics directly on transactional data, providing real-time insights without the need for data replication or batch processing.

The key components of SAP S/4HANA analytics architecture include:

11.2.1 SAP HANA In-Memory Database

At the heart of SAP S/4HANA's analytics capabilities is the **SAP HANA** in-memory database. Unlike traditional databases, which store data on disk and retrieve it as needed, SAP HANA stores all data in memory (RAM), allowing for near-instantaneous data access and processing. This enables users to perform complex queries, generate reports, and run analytics on large datasets in real time.

Key benefits of the SAP HANA in-memory database include:

- **Real-Time Analytics**: SAP HANA allows users to analyze data as soon as it is created, providing real-time insights into business performance.

- **Reduced Data Redundancy**: The in-memory architecture eliminates the need for aggregate and index tables, reducing data redundancy and improving the efficiency of data management.
- **High-Performance Processing**: The combination of columnar data storage and in-memory computing allows SAP HANA to process complex queries and analytics much faster than traditional databases.

11.2.2 Core Data Services (CDS) Views

**Core Data Services (CDS)** views are a key component of SAP S/4HANA's analytics architecture. CDS views provide a semantic layer for defining and modeling data in a way that supports both transactional and analytical processing. CDS views allow businesses to create virtual data models, which can be used for reporting and analytics without the need for data replication or physical tables.

Key features of CDS views include:

- **Virtual Data Models**: CDS views allow users to define virtual data models that provide a unified view of data from multiple sources. These models can be used for real-time reporting and analytics without impacting transactional performance.

- **Reusable Data Definitions**: CDS views can be reused across different applications, making it easier to standardize data models and reporting across the organization.
- **Integration with SAP Fiori**: CDS views can be consumed by SAP Fiori apps, enabling users to view and interact with reports and dashboards directly within the SAP S/4HANA user interface.

11.2.3 Embedded Analytics

**Embedded analytics** is one of the most powerful features of SAP S/4HANA. Unlike traditional business intelligence systems, where data is extracted and analyzed in a separate environment, SAP S/4HANA integrates analytics directly into the core system. This means that users can generate real-time reports and dashboards based on live transactional data without the need for data extraction or replication.

Key benefits of embedded analytics include:

- **Real-Time Insights**: Embedded analytics allows users to access real-time data and insights as part of their daily operations. For example, a sales manager can view live sales data and adjust strategies on the fly, while a financial analyst can monitor cash flow in real time.
- **Actionable Dashboards**: Embedded analytics provides interactive dashboards that display key

performance indicators (KPIs), trends, and insights in a visually intuitive format. These dashboards are integrated into the SAP Fiori interface, making it easy for users to interact with data and take immediate action.
- **Seamless Integration**: Embedded analytics integrates seamlessly with other SAP S/4HANA modules, such as Finance (FI), Sales and Distribution (SD), and Materials Management (MM), providing a unified view of business data across the organization.

11.2.4 SAP Fiori for Analytics

**SAP Fiori** is the user experience platform for SAP S/4HANA, and it plays a critical role in delivering analytics to end users. Fiori provides a modern, role-based, and responsive user interface that allows users to access reports, dashboards, and analytics from any device, including desktops, tablets, and smartphones.

Key features of SAP Fiori for analytics include:

- **Role-Based Dashboards**: Fiori apps are designed to provide role-based dashboards that display the most relevant data for each user. For example, a finance manager's dashboard might display key financial metrics, while a warehouse manager's dashboard might focus on inventory levels and stock movements.

- **KPI Tiles**: Fiori's tile-based design allows users to display key performance indicators (KPIs) on their home screen. These KPI tiles provide real-time updates and can be drilled down to explore underlying data.
- **Interactive Reports and Visualizations**: Fiori provides users with interactive reports and visualizations that allow them to explore data in depth. Users can filter data, drill down into specific metrics, and generate custom reports on demand.

## 11.3 Key Features of SAP S/4HANA Analytics

SAP S/4HANA analytics offers a wide range of features designed to help businesses gain insights into their operations and drive better decision-making. These features include real-time reporting, predictive analytics, and advanced visualizations.

### 11.3.1 Real-Time Reporting

One of the most significant advantages of SAP S/4HANA analytics is its ability to provide **real-time reporting**. Traditional reporting systems often rely on batch processing, where data is updated periodically, leading to delays in accessing the latest information. In contrast, SAP S/4HANA allows users to generate reports based on live transactional data, ensuring that they always have the most up-to-date information.

Real-time reporting capabilities include:

- **Predefined Reports**: SAP S/4HANA includes a wide range of predefined reports across different functional areas, such as finance, sales, procurement, and production. These reports provide users with ready-to-use insights without the need for complex configuration.
- **Ad-Hoc Reporting**: Users can create ad-hoc reports by defining custom filters, parameters, and data views. This flexibility allows users to generate insights on the fly without relying on IT or technical resources.
- **Drill-Down Capabilities**: SAP S/4HANA's reports allow users to drill down into specific data points to explore underlying details. For example, a user viewing a financial report can drill down into individual transactions to understand the source of variances or discrepancies.

11.3.2 Predictive Analytics

**Predictive analytics** is another key feature of SAP S/4HANA, allowing businesses to forecast future outcomes based on historical data. Predictive analytics helps organizations anticipate trends, identify risks, and optimize their operations.

Key predictive analytics capabilities include:

- **Forecasting**: SAP S/4HANA can generate forecasts based on historical trends and patterns. For example, sales teams can use predictive analytics to forecast future demand, while finance teams can forecast cash flow or profitability based on historical performance.
- **Machine Learning Integration**: SAP S/4HANA integrates with **SAP Leonardo** and other machine learning platforms to enhance predictive analytics with advanced algorithms. This enables businesses to build more accurate predictive models and automate decision-making processes.
- **Risk Analysis**: Predictive analytics can be used to identify potential risks, such as supply chain disruptions or financial shortfalls, allowing businesses to take proactive measures to mitigate these risks.

11.3.3 Data Visualization and Dashboards

SAP S/4HANA provides advanced **data visualization** tools that make it easy for users to interpret complex data. Dashboards and visualizations present data in a clear and intuitive format, helping users understand trends, identify patterns, and make informed decisions.

Key features of data visualization and dashboards include:

- **Interactive Dashboards**: Users can interact with dashboards by filtering data, selecting time ranges, or drilling down into specific metrics. This allows users to explore data dynamically and uncover insights that may not be apparent in static reports.
- **Charts and Graphs**: SAP S/4HANA supports a wide variety of chart types, including bar charts, line charts, pie charts, and scatter plots, making it easy to visualize different types of data.
- **Customizable Dashboards**: Users can customize their dashboards by adding or removing KPIs, changing layouts, and configuring alerts. This ensures that each user's dashboard is tailored to their specific needs and responsibilities.

**11.4 Use Cases for SAP S/4HANA Analytics**

SAP S/4HANA's analytics capabilities are applicable across a wide range of business functions and industries. Below are some key use cases where SAP S/4HANA analytics delivers significant value:

11.4.1 Financial Performance Monitoring

Finance teams can use SAP S/4HANA analytics to monitor key financial metrics such as revenue, expenses, cash flow, and profitability in real time. With embedded analytics, financial managers can track their organization's financial health and respond quickly to any variances or issues.

Key use cases in finance include:

- **Real-Time Cash Flow Monitoring**: SAP S/4HANA enables finance teams to monitor cash inflows and outflows in real time, helping them optimize liquidity management and ensure that the business remains financially stable.
- **Profitability Analysis**: Financial analysts can use profitability reports to evaluate the performance of different business units, product lines, or regions, helping them identify the most profitable areas of the business.
- **Financial Close Process**: During the financial close process, SAP S/4HANA's real-time reporting capabilities help finance teams generate accurate and timely financial statements, reducing the time required to close the books.

11.4.2 Sales and Revenue Analytics

Sales teams can leverage SAP S/4HANA analytics to track sales performance, monitor customer behavior, and optimize pricing strategies. The system provides real-time insights into sales revenue, customer orders, and market trends.

Key use cases in sales include:

- **Sales Performance Dashboards**: Sales managers can track key sales metrics, such as revenue growth, order fulfillment rates, and sales by region or product. This helps them identify high-performing sales channels and areas for improvement.
- **Customer Segmentation**: SAP S/4HANA analytics allows sales teams to segment customers based on purchasing behavior, enabling targeted marketing and personalized customer engagement.
- **Revenue Forecasting**: Sales teams can use predictive analytics to forecast future revenue based on historical sales data, market conditions, and customer trends.

11.4.3 Supply Chain Optimization

Supply chain managers can use SAP S/4HANA analytics to gain visibility into inventory levels, supplier performance, and production efficiency. Real-time analytics helps businesses optimize their supply chain operations by identifying bottlenecks, reducing lead times, and minimizing stockouts.

Key use cases in supply chain management include:

- **Inventory Optimization**: Real-time inventory reports allow supply chain managers to track stock levels across multiple warehouses and ensure that inventory is optimized to meet customer demand.
- **Supplier Performance Monitoring**: SAP S/4HANA analytics provides insights into supplier performance, helping procurement teams evaluate supplier reliability, delivery times, and cost-effectiveness.
- **Production Efficiency**: By tracking production metrics in real time, businesses can identify inefficiencies in their manufacturing processes and make adjustments to improve production output.

## 11.5 Best Practices for Implementing SAP S/4HANA Analytics

To maximize the value of SAP S/4HANA analytics, businesses should follow best practices for implementation and use.

### 11.5.1 Define Key Metrics and KPIs

Before implementing SAP S/4HANA analytics, it is essential to define the key metrics and KPIs that will be used to measure performance. This ensures that the system is configured to track the most relevant data for each business function and that users have access to the insights they need.

### 11.5.2 Leverage Real-Time Reporting

Take full advantage of SAP S/4HANA's real-time reporting capabilities. Regularly monitor KPIs and use real-time dashboards to make data-driven decisions in day-to-day operations. Encourage users to interact with data dynamically, using filters and drill-down capabilities to explore insights.

### 11.5.3 Integrate Predictive Analytics

Use predictive analytics to forecast future outcomes and identify potential risks or opportunities. Integrating machine learning and advanced algorithms can help businesses make more accurate predictions and optimize their operations based on data-driven forecasts.

### 11.5.4 Customize Dashboards for Different Roles

Ensure that each user's dashboard is customized to their role and responsibilities. Role-based dashboards provide users with the most relevant data and insights, improving decision-making and productivity.

### 11.6 Conclusion: Unlocking the Power of Data with SAP S/4HANA Analytics

SAP S/4HANA analytics offers businesses a powerful set of tools for gaining real-time insights, optimizing operations, and driving data-driven decision-making. By integrating analytics directly into the core ERP system, SAP S/4HANA enables users to access real-time reports, dashboards, and predictive insights without relying on separate BI systems or data warehouses.

In this chapter, we explored the key components of SAP S/4HANA analytics, including the SAP HANA in-memory database, Core Data Services (CDS) views, and embedded analytics. We also covered how businesses can use these tools to monitor financial performance, optimize sales and supply chain operations, and forecast future outcomes.

In the next chapter, we will explore **Integrating SAP S/4HANA with Other Systems** in detail.

# Chapter 12: Integrating SAP S/4HANA with Other Systems

## 12.1 Introduction to SAP S/4HANA Integration

SAP S/4HANA is a comprehensive enterprise resource planning (ERP) system designed to streamline and integrate an organization's core business processes. However, for many businesses, SAP S/4HANA is only one part of a broader IT ecosystem. Many organizations rely on various external systems and third-party applications for specific functions, such as customer relationship management (CRM), supply chain management (SCM), e-commerce, and data analytics. Ensuring seamless integration between SAP S/4HANA and these external systems is critical for maximizing efficiency, enhancing data flow, and improving decision-making across the enterprise.

In this chapter, we will explore the different methods of integrating SAP S/4HANA with other systems, the tools and technologies available for integration, and the best practices for ensuring successful integration. Whether you are connecting SAP S/4HANA with legacy systems, cloud platforms, or external databases, understanding the available integration approaches is key to building a cohesive and interconnected business landscape.

**12.2 Integration Options for SAP S/4HANA**

SAP S/4HANA supports a variety of integration methods that cater to different business needs and IT environments. The primary integration options available for SAP S/4HANA include:

12.2.1 SAP Integration Suite

The **SAP Integration Suite** (formerly known as SAP Cloud Platform Integration) is SAP's flagship integration platform. It provides a comprehensive set of tools and services for integrating SAP S/4HANA with other SAP applications, third-party systems, and cloud services.

Key features of SAP Integration Suite include:

- **Prebuilt Integration Content**: SAP Integration Suite offers prebuilt integration content for connecting SAP S/4HANA with other systems, such as SAP SuccessFactors, SAP Ariba, SAP Concur, and third-party applications like Salesforce. These integration packages simplify the implementation process by providing ready-to-use templates and connectors.
- **APIs and Web Services**: The platform supports APIs, web services, and RESTful integration, allowing businesses to connect SAP S/4HANA with virtually any external system. SAP provides a vast library of APIs through the **SAP API**

**Business Hub**, enabling businesses to integrate core processes like sales, procurement, finance, and logistics with other systems.

- **Hybrid Integration**: SAP Integration Suite supports both on-premise and cloud integration, making it suitable for businesses operating in hybrid IT environments. It allows businesses to connect legacy on-premise systems with modern cloud-based applications.

- **Security and Governance**: The platform provides robust security features, including data encryption, access control, and monitoring tools to ensure that integrations are secure and compliant with industry regulations.

12.2.2 SAP Process Orchestration (PO)

**SAP Process Orchestration** (PO) is an on-premise integration tool that helps businesses automate and manage business processes across multiple systems. It is ideal for integrating SAP S/4HANA with legacy systems and other on-premise applications.

Key features of SAP Process Orchestration include:

- **Business Process Automation**: SAP PO enables businesses to automate complex workflows and integrate business processes across different systems. It supports integration scenarios such as order-to-cash, procure-to-pay, and production planning.

- **Enterprise Service Bus (ESB)**: SAP PO acts as an enterprise service bus (ESB), allowing different systems to communicate through a centralized platform. It supports various communication protocols, including SOAP, REST, and HTTP, making it easy to connect SAP S/4HANA with other systems.
- **Message Transformation**: SAP PO includes tools for transforming data between different formats (e.g., XML, JSON, CSV), enabling seamless communication between SAP S/4HANA and external systems with different data structures.

12.2.3 SAP Business Technology Platform (BTP)

The **SAP Business Technology Platform (BTP)** is a cloud-based platform that supports integration, data management, and application development. BTP provides a set of services that enable businesses to connect SAP S/4HANA with cloud applications, external databases, and third-party systems.

Key features of SAP BTP include:

- **SAP Extension Suite**: BTP offers an extension suite that allows businesses to build custom applications, microservices, and extensions on top of SAP S/4HANA. These applications can be integrated with external systems to extend the functionality of SAP S/4HANA.

- **Data Integration**: SAP BTP provides tools for integrating data from SAP S/4HANA with external databases and data lakes. This integration is useful for organizations that require advanced analytics, machine learning, or data science capabilities.
- **Event-Driven Integration**: SAP BTP supports event-driven integration, enabling systems to communicate based on specific business events (e.g., a sales order being created or a purchase order being approved). This reduces latency in business processes and ensures that systems are updated in real time.

12.2.4 SAP API Business Hub

The **SAP API Business Hub** is a central repository for SAP and partner APIs. It provides access to a wide range of APIs for integrating SAP S/4HANA with other SAP solutions (e.g., SAP Ariba, SAP SuccessFactors) and third-party applications.

Key features of the SAP API Business Hub include:

- **Prebuilt APIs**: SAP API Business Hub offers prebuilt APIs for common business processes such as sales order creation, inventory management, and financial reporting. These APIs can be used to connect SAP S/4HANA with external applications quickly and efficiently.

- **API Documentation**: The platform provides comprehensive documentation for each API, including usage examples, request and response formats, and authentication methods.
- **Integration with Third-Party Applications**: In addition to SAP APIs, the platform also includes connectors for integrating with popular third-party applications such as Salesforce, Microsoft Dynamics, and Google Cloud.

12.2.5 SAP Data Intelligence

**SAP Data Intelligence** is a comprehensive data management solution that supports data integration, orchestration, and transformation across multiple systems. It is designed for businesses that need to integrate SAP S/4HANA with external data sources and data lakes for advanced analytics, AI, and machine learning.

Key features of SAP Data Intelligence include:

- **Data Pipelines**: SAP Data Intelligence allows businesses to create data pipelines that move and transform data between SAP S/4HANA and external systems, ensuring that data is synchronized in real time.

- **Data Governance**: The platform provides tools for managing data quality, ensuring that data is accurate and consistent across all integrated systems.
- **Machine Learning Integration**: SAP Data Intelligence supports the integration of machine learning models and algorithms, enabling businesses to apply predictive analytics and AI to their data.

## 12.3 Common Integration Scenarios

SAP S/4HANA integration can be applied across a wide range of business processes and systems. Below are some of the most common integration scenarios that businesses encounter when integrating SAP S/4HANA with other systems.

### 12.3.1 Integration with Customer Relationship Management (CRM) Systems

Many organizations use CRM systems like **SAP Customer Experience (CX)** or **Salesforce** to manage customer interactions, sales, and marketing activities. Integrating CRM systems with SAP S/4HANA ensures that customer data flows seamlessly between the front-office and back-office systems.

Key benefits of CRM integration include:

- **360-Degree View of Customers**: Integration allows businesses to maintain a unified view of customer data, including sales history, purchase orders, and service requests, across both CRM and ERP systems.
- **Improved Sales and Service Processes**: Sales and customer service teams can access real-time inventory data, pricing information, and order status directly from SAP S/4HANA, improving the accuracy and efficiency of sales and service processes.
- **Automated Order Processing**: When a sales order is created in the CRM system, it can be automatically transferred to SAP S/4HANA for fulfillment, invoicing, and financial posting.

12.3.2 Integration with E-Commerce Platforms

Businesses that operate online stores often need to integrate their e-commerce platforms (such as **Shopify**, **Magento**, or **SAP Commerce Cloud**) with SAP S/4HANA to manage orders, inventory, and fulfillment.

Key benefits of e-commerce integration include:

- **Real-Time Inventory Updates**: Integration ensures that inventory levels are updated in real time, preventing stockouts or overselling of products.

- **Automated Order Fulfillment**: When a customer places an order through the e-commerce platform, it can be automatically transferred to SAP S/4HANA for processing, ensuring that the order is fulfilled quickly and accurately.
- **Financial Reconciliation**: Integration ensures that sales revenue from the e-commerce platform is posted directly to the financial accounts in SAP S/4HANA, streamlining financial reconciliation.

12.3.3 Integration with Supply Chain Management (SCM) Systems

Many organizations use third-party supply chain management (SCM) systems to optimize their procurement, logistics, and warehouse operations. Integrating SCM systems with SAP S/4HANA ensures that supply chain data is synchronized with the organization's core ERP system.

Key benefits of SCM integration include:

- **Improved Demand Planning**: By integrating SCM systems with SAP S/4HANA, businesses can align their demand planning processes with real-time sales and production data, improving accuracy and reducing inventory costs.

- **Streamlined Procurement Processes**: When purchase requisitions are created in SAP S/4HANA, they can be automatically transferred to the SCM system for supplier evaluation and order fulfillment.
- **Enhanced Visibility**: Integration provides real-time visibility into the entire supply chain, allowing businesses to monitor inventory levels, supplier performance, and logistics operations more effectively.

12.3.4 Integration with Financial Systems

Many organizations use external financial systems, such as **SAP Concur** for expense management or **Treasury Management Systems (TMS)** for managing cash flow and investments. Integrating these systems with SAP S/4HANA ensures that financial data is consistently reflected in the organization's general ledger and financial reports.

Key benefits of financial system integration include:

- **Automated Expense Reporting**: When employees submit expense reports through an external system (such as SAP Concur), the expenses can be automatically posted to SAP S/4HANA's financial accounts for reconciliation and reporting.

- **Real-Time Cash Flow Management**: Integration with treasury systems allows businesses to manage cash flow, investments, and foreign exchange transactions in real time, ensuring that financial data is always up to date.
- **Enhanced Financial Reporting**: By integrating external financial systems with SAP S/4HANA, businesses can consolidate financial data from multiple sources, improving the accuracy and timeliness of financial reporting.

## 12.4 Best Practices for Integrating SAP S/4HANA with Other Systems

To ensure successful integration of SAP S/4HANA with other systems, businesses should follow best practices to minimize risks, reduce complexity, and ensure data consistency.

### 12.4.1 Define Clear Integration Requirements

Before starting any integration project, it is important to define the specific requirements and objectives of the integration. This includes identifying which systems need to be integrated, what data needs to be exchanged, and how the integration will support business processes. Clear requirements help avoid scope creep and ensure that the integration project delivers the expected outcomes.

### 12.4.2 Choose the Right Integration Tools

SAP offers a range of integration tools, including SAP Integration Suite, SAP Process Orchestration, and SAP API Business Hub. It is essential to choose the right integration tool based on your business needs, IT environment, and the complexity of the integration. For example, cloud-based businesses may prefer SAP Integration Suite, while organizations with legacy systems may rely on SAP Process Orchestration.

### 12.4.3 Ensure Data Consistency and Integrity

When integrating SAP S/4HANA with other systems, it is critical to ensure that data remains consistent across all systems. This includes setting up data validation rules, monitoring data synchronization, and resolving any data conflicts or discrepancies that arise during the integration process. Maintaining data integrity is essential for ensuring accurate reporting and decision-making.

### 12.4.4 Test Integrations Thoroughly

Before going live with any integration, it is important to thoroughly test the integration in a controlled environment. This includes testing data flows, system performance, and error handling to ensure that the integration works as expected under various conditions.

Comprehensive testing reduces the risk of system failures and ensures a smooth transition to production.

### 12.4.5 Monitor and Maintain Integrations

Once the integration is live, it is important to monitor its performance regularly and address any issues that arise. This includes tracking data exchange volumes, monitoring system performance, and resolving integration errors or bottlenecks. Regular maintenance ensures that integrations continue to function efficiently and that data flows remain consistent.

## 12.5 Conclusion: Building a Connected Business with SAP S/4HANA Integration

Integrating SAP S/4HANA with other systems is essential for building a connected and cohesive IT environment. By leveraging SAP's powerful integration tools, businesses can streamline processes, improve data visibility, and optimize operations across the entire organization. Whether you are connecting SAP S/4HANA with CRM systems, e-commerce platforms, financial systems, or supply chain management solutions, understanding the available integration options and best practices is critical for ensuring a successful integration.

In this chapter, we explored the key methods for integrating SAP S/4HANA with other systems, including

SAP Integration Suite, SAP Process Orchestration, and SAP API Business Hub. We also discussed common integration scenarios and best practices for ensuring seamless data flow and operational efficiency. In the next chapter, we will dive into **Data Migration in SAP S/4HANA** and discuss how businesses can transition their data from legacy systems to SAP S/4HANA while ensuring data quality and consistency.

In the next chapter, we will explore **Data Migration in SAP S/4HANA**, discussing how businesses can efficiently transition their data from legacy systems to SAP S/4HANA while ensuring data accuracy and consistency.

# Chapter 13: Data Migration to SAP S/4HANA

### 13.1 Introduction to Data Migration in SAP S/4HANA

Data migration is a critical part of any enterprise resource planning (ERP) implementation or upgrade, and SAP S/4HANA is no exception. Moving data from legacy systems to SAP S/4HANA is essential to ensure business continuity, maintain data integrity, and enable the organization to leverage the full capabilities of the new system. Data migration can be complex, requiring careful planning, data cleansing, mapping, and testing to ensure that all relevant data is accurately transferred and that business processes remain uninterrupted.

This chapter will explore the key steps, tools, and best practices for migrating data to SAP S/4HANA. We will cover the data migration lifecycle, the SAP-provided tools, such as the **SAP S/4HANA Migration Cockpit**, and strategies to ensure a smooth transition from legacy systems to SAP S/4HANA.

### 13.2 Overview of the Data Migration Lifecycle

The data migration lifecycle for SAP S/4HANA consists of several phases, each of which plays a crucial role in ensuring that data is transferred accurately and efficiently. These phases include planning, data extraction, data transformation, data loading, and testing.

13.2.1 Phase 1: Planning and Preparation

The first phase of any data migration project is planning and preparation. This phase involves understanding the scope of the migration, defining the data that needs to be transferred, and establishing a timeline for the migration process.

Key steps in the planning and preparation phase include:

- **Identifying Data Objects**: Determine which data objects need to be migrated, such as master data (e.g., customers, vendors, materials) and transactional data (e.g., sales orders, purchase orders, financial transactions).
- **Defining Migration Scope**: Decide which data will be migrated to SAP S/4HANA and which data may be archived or left behind. Some historical data may not be needed in the new system, while critical transactional data must be included.
- **Data Migration Strategy**: Establish whether you will perform a **big bang** migration (where all data is migrated in one go) or a **phased migration** (where data is migrated in stages).

- **Setting Timelines**: Develop a timeline for the migration process, including key milestones such as data extraction, data transformation, initial load, and final cutover.

13.2.2 Phase 2: Data Extraction

The second phase involves extracting data from legacy systems or external sources that need to be migrated into SAP S/4HANA. This phase requires identifying the correct data sources, ensuring data quality, and extracting the data in a format that can be processed by the migration tools.

Key considerations for data extraction include:

- **Data Source Identification**: Identify all legacy systems, databases, and external applications that store the data to be migrated.
- **Data Cleansing**: Cleanse the data to ensure accuracy, completeness, and consistency. This includes removing duplicates, correcting errors, and standardizing data formats. Data cleansing is crucial for ensuring data quality in SAP S/4HANA.
- **Data Formatting**: Extract data in a structured format (such as CSV, XML, or Excel) that can be processed by the migration tools.

13.2.3 Phase 3: Data Transformation and Mapping

Once the data has been extracted, it needs to be transformed and mapped to the data structures in SAP S/4HANA. This phase ensures that the data fits into the predefined fields and formats required by SAP S/4HANA.

Key steps in data transformation and mapping include:

- **Data Mapping**: Map the data fields from the legacy system to the corresponding fields in SAP S/4HANA. For example, customer records in the legacy system must be mapped to the appropriate customer master fields in SAP S/4HANA.
- **Data Transformation**: Convert data into the correct format required by SAP S/4HANA. For example, date formats, units of measurement, and currency formats may need to be transformed to align with SAP standards.
- **Business Rules Application**: Apply business rules and validation logic to ensure that the data meets the specific requirements of the business processes in SAP S/4HANA.

13.2.4 Phase 4: Data Loading

The fourth phase involves loading the transformed and mapped data into SAP S/4HANA. This is typically done in stages, starting with a test load, followed by an initial load, and finally the production load during the system cutover.

Key steps in data loading include:

- **Test Load**: Perform a test load in a sandbox or quality environment to ensure that the data is transferred correctly. The test load helps identify any issues with data mapping, formatting, or system performance.
- **Initial Load**: After successful testing, perform the initial data load into the SAP S/4HANA production environment. This is typically done before the final cutover, allowing businesses to validate the data in the new system.
- **Production Load (Cutover)**: The final data load is performed during the system cutover, where the legacy system is decommissioned, and SAP S/4HANA becomes the system of record. This load includes all remaining transactional data and ensures that the system is ready for business operations.

13.2.5 Phase 5: Data Validation and Testing

The final phase of the data migration process involves validating the data and testing the system to ensure that the migration was successful. This phase ensures that the data is accurate, complete, and fully functional in the new system.

Key steps in data validation and testing include:

- **Data Reconciliation**: Compare data between the legacy system and SAP S/4HANA to ensure that all records have been migrated accurately. This includes checking master data, transactional data, and financial balances.
- **Functional Testing**: Perform functional testing of key business processes (such as order-to-cash, procure-to-pay, and financial reporting) to ensure that the data is correctly integrated and supports the new system's operations.
- **User Acceptance Testing (UAT)**: Conduct user acceptance testing to validate that the migrated data supports the day-to-day activities of end-users and that the system meets business requirements.

**13.3 Tools for Data Migration in SAP S/4HANA**

SAP provides a variety of tools to support data migration to SAP S/4HANA. These tools are designed to streamline the migration process, reduce manual effort, and ensure data quality.

13.3.1 SAP S/4HANA Migration Cockpit

The **SAP S/4HANA Migration Cockpit** is a user-friendly tool designed to simplify the data migration process. It provides predefined migration templates for various data objects and automates many aspects of data extraction, mapping, and loading.

Key features of the SAP S/4HANA Migration Cockpit include:

- **Predefined Migration Objects**: The migration cockpit includes predefined templates for common data objects such as customers, vendors, materials, and financial transactions. These templates include predefined mapping rules and data structures, reducing the complexity of data migration.
- **No Coding Required**: The migration cockpit is designed for business users and requires no technical coding skills. Users can upload data files (such as Excel or CSV files) into the cockpit, map the data fields, and execute the migration without the need for custom development.
- **Automated Data Validation**: The tool includes built-in validation rules that check the data for errors before it is loaded into SAP S/4HANA. This ensures that only clean and accurate data is migrated.

- **Real-Time Monitoring**: The migration cockpit provides real-time monitoring of the migration process, allowing users to track the progress of data loads, resolve errors, and ensure that the migration stays on track.

13.3.2 SAP Data Services

**SAP Data Services** is a powerful data integration and migration tool that provides advanced data extraction, transformation, and loading (ETL) capabilities. It is ideal for complex data migration projects where data needs to be extracted from multiple sources and transformed into complex formats.

Key features of SAP Data Services include:

- **Complex Data Transformations**: SAP Data Services supports complex data transformations, allowing businesses to cleanse, transform, and enrich data before it is migrated to SAP S/4HANA.
- **Data Quality Management**: The tool includes features for managing data quality, such as duplication, address validation, and data enrichment. This ensures that only high-quality data is migrated to SAP S/4HANA.
- **Integration with Legacy Systems**: SAP Data Services can connect to a wide range of legacy systems, databases, and external applications,

making it a versatile tool for migrating data from various sources.

13.3.3 SAP Landscape Transformation (SLT)

**SAP Landscape Transformation (SLT)** is a tool used for real-time data replication and migration. It is particularly useful for organizations that need to replicate data from SAP or non-SAP systems into SAP S/4HANA in real time.

Key features of SAP Landscape Transformation include:

- **Real-Time Data Replication**: SLT allows businesses to replicate data from legacy systems to SAP S/4HANA in real time, ensuring that data is synchronized during the migration process.
- **Minimized Downtime**: SLT minimizes system downtime during the migration process by replicating data continuously, reducing the need for a full system shutdown.
- **Cross-System Data Integration**: SLT supports the integration of data from multiple systems, making it ideal for businesses with complex IT landscapes that need to migrate data from different environments.

13.3.4 SAP Information Steward

**SAP Information Steward** is a data governance and quality management tool that helps businesses ensure data accuracy and consistency during the migration process.

Key features of SAP Information Steward include:

- **Data Quality Validation**: SAP Information Steward provides tools for validating the quality of data before it is migrated to SAP S/4HANA. It checks for data completeness, consistency, and accuracy, ensuring that the data meets the organization's quality standards.
- **Data Lineage and Impact Analysis**: The tool provides insights into data lineage, showing where data originated and how it has been transformed. This helps businesses track the flow of data during the migration process and understand the impact of changes.

## 13.4 Data Migration Challenges and How to Overcome Them

Data migration can be a complex and challenging process. However, by understanding the potential challenges and implementing best practices, businesses can minimize risks and ensure a smooth migration to SAP S/4HANA.

### 13.4.1 Data Quality Issues

One of the most common challenges in data migration is poor data quality. Inaccurate, incomplete, or outdated data can lead to operational issues and inaccurate reporting in the new system.

**Solution**: Implement a comprehensive data cleansing process before the migration. Use tools like SAP Information Steward to validate and cleanse the data, ensuring that only high-quality data is migrated to SAP S/4HANA.

### 13.4.2 Data Mapping Complexities

Data mapping can be complex, especially when migrating from legacy systems with different data structures. Incorrect mappings can lead to errors in the migrated data.

**Solution**: Carefully map data fields between the legacy system and SAP S/4HANA. Use predefined templates in the SAP S/4HANA Migration Cockpit to simplify the mapping process, and involve subject matter experts to ensure that data is mapped correctly.

### 13.4.3 System Downtime and Business Disruption

Data migration often requires system downtime, which can disrupt business operations. Minimizing downtime is critical for ensuring business continuity.

**Solution**: Use tools like SAP Landscape Transformation (SLT) to replicate data in real time, minimizing downtime during the migration process. Plan the final data load and cutover during a low-activity period to reduce the impact on business operations.

### 13.4.4 Incomplete Data Migration

If data is not migrated completely or accurately, it can lead to missing records or incorrect data in the new system, affecting business processes.

**Solution**: Perform thorough data validation and reconciliation to ensure that all data has been migrated correctly. Use tools like the SAP S/4HANA Migration Cockpit to validate data before it is loaded into the new system, and conduct functional testing to ensure that key business processes work as expected.

## 13.5 Best Practices for Data Migration to SAP S/4HANA

To ensure a successful data migration to SAP S/4HANA, businesses should follow best practices that minimize risks and maximize efficiency.

### 13.5.1 Start with Data Cleansing

Before migrating data, perform a thorough data cleansing process to ensure that only accurate and relevant data is migrated to SAP S/4HANA. This reduces the risk of migrating outdated or incorrect data, improving the overall quality of the system.

### 13.5.2 Use SAP's Predefined Migration Tools

Leverage SAP's predefined migration tools, such as the SAP S/4HANA Migration Cockpit, to simplify the migration process. These tools include predefined templates and automated workflows that reduce manual effort and ensure consistency.

### 13.5.3 Perform Multiple Test Migrations

Conduct multiple test migrations in a sandbox or quality environment to identify and resolve issues before the final cutover. Test migrations allow businesses to validate data mappings, identify system performance issues, and ensure that the data is loaded correctly.

### 13.5.4 Monitor and Validate Data Throughout the Process

Monitor the migration process closely, and validate the data at every stage to ensure accuracy. This includes comparing data between the legacy system and SAP

S/4HANA, conducting functional testing, and involving end-users in the validation process.

13.5.5 Plan for Post-Migration Support

After the migration is complete, provide ongoing support to address any issues that arise during the stabilization period. This includes resolving data discrepancies, providing training for end-users, and monitoring system performance.

## 13.6 Conclusion: Ensuring a Successful Data Migration to SAP S/4HANA

Data migration is a crucial part of any SAP S/4HANA implementation. By carefully planning the migration process, using SAP's powerful migration tools, and following best practices for data cleansing, mapping, and validation, businesses can ensure a smooth transition from legacy systems to SAP S/4HANA.

In this chapter, we covered the key phases of data migration, available tools, and common challenges. By addressing these challenges and following best practices, businesses can ensure a successful migration and unlock the full potential of SAP S/4HANA.

In the next chapter, we will explore **SAP Activate Methodology** in detail.

# Chapter 14: Exploring SAP Activate Methodology

## 14.1 Introduction to SAP Activate Methodology

The **SAP Activate Methodology** is a structured and agile framework designed to streamline and simplify the implementation of SAP solutions, including **SAP S/4HANA**. It provides a standardized approach for planning, implementing, and managing SAP projects, ensuring that organizations can deploy SAP systems efficiently while minimizing risks and disruptions to business operations. SAP Activate combines **best practices**, **guided configurations**, and an **agile project management approach** to help businesses transition from legacy systems to SAP S/4HANA, either in the cloud, on-premise, or hybrid environments.

SAP Activate is designed to be flexible, enabling organizations to adapt the methodology to their specific needs. It is built around a lifecycle that includes well-defined phases, workstreams, and deliverables. In this chapter, we will explore the core components of the SAP Activate Methodology, its phases, and how businesses can use it to successfully implement SAP S/4HANA.

**14.2 Core Components of SAP Activate Methodology**

The SAP Activate Methodology consists of three key components: **SAP Best Practices**, **Guided Configuration**, and **Agile Project Management**. These components work together to accelerate the implementation process, reduce complexity, and ensure that businesses are adopting proven practices that align with their industry and business model.

14.2.1 SAP Best Practices

**SAP Best Practices** are pre-configured business processes that have been developed based on industry standards and the experience SAP has gained from working with thousands of customers. These best practices provide a blueprint for implementing common business processes, ensuring that organizations can quickly adopt SAP S/4HANA without having to build configurations from scratch.

Key features of SAP Best Practices include:

- **Preconfigured Business Processes**: SAP Best Practices cover end-to-end business processes such as order-to-cash, procure-to-pay, financial management, supply chain management, and more. These pre-configured processes are tailored to different industries, enabling businesses to adopt industry-specific solutions.

- **Accelerated Deployment**: By leveraging SAP Best Practices, businesses can speed up the deployment of SAP S/4HANA, as the majority of configurations are already in place. This reduces the time and effort required to design and configure the system.
- **Customizable**: While SAP Best Practices provide a standard set of configurations, they are also highly customizable. Businesses can adjust the pre-configured settings to meet their specific requirements or add new functionality as needed.

14.2.2 Guided Configuration

**Guided Configuration** is a tool within SAP S/4HANA that provides a structured and intuitive way to configure the system based on SAP Best Practices. It simplifies the process of tailoring SAP S/4HANA to the specific needs of an organization by offering guided steps, predefined content, and automated checks.

Key features of Guided Configuration include:

- **Predefined Configurations**: The tool provides predefined configurations that are based on SAP Best Practices. This allows businesses to quickly set up core business processes without the need for extensive technical expertise.

- **Step-by-Step Guidance**: Guided Configuration walks users through the configuration process in a structured and logical manner. Each step is clearly defined, and users are guided through activities such as defining organizational structures, setting up master data, and configuring system parameters.
- **Real-Time Validation**: As users configure the system, Guided Configuration performs real-time validations to ensure that configurations are consistent and error-free. This reduces the risk of configuration errors and ensures that the system is set up correctly from the start.

14.2.3 Agile Project Management

The SAP Activate Methodology incorporates **agile project management** principles, which enable organizations to implement SAP solutions in short, iterative cycles. Agile methodologies emphasize flexibility, collaboration, and incremental progress, allowing teams to deliver value faster and respond to changing requirements throughout the project lifecycle.

Key features of Agile Project Management in SAP Activate include:

- **Sprint-Based Approach**: SAP Activate uses a sprint-based approach to implementation, where work is divided into short, focused

167

iterations (called sprints). Each sprint typically lasts two to four weeks and focuses on delivering a specific set of deliverables, such as configuring a particular business process or migrating data.

- **Continuous Feedback**: Agile emphasizes continuous feedback from stakeholders and end-users. Regular check-ins, reviews, and retrospectives ensure that any issues or changes in requirements are identified early and addressed promptly.
- **Cross-Functional Collaboration**: Agile project management encourages collaboration across different teams, including IT, business users, and external consultants. This ensures that all stakeholders are aligned on project goals and that business requirements are accurately reflected in the system configuration.

**14.3 Phases of the SAP Activate Methodology**

The SAP Activate Methodology is structured into six distinct phases: **Discover**, **Prepare**, **Explore**, **Realize**, **Deploy**, and **Run**. Each phase represents a different stage in the project lifecycle and includes specific deliverables, tasks, and milestones.

### 14.3.1 Phase 1: Discover

The **Discover** phase is the first step in the SAP Activate Methodology, and it focuses on defining the overall project strategy and objectives. During this phase, the organization assesses its business needs, evaluates the benefits of SAP S/4HANA, and determines the scope of the implementation.

Key activities in the Discover phase include:

- **Project Vision**: Define the project's vision, goals, and expected outcomes. This includes identifying the business processes that will be transformed and the key benefits of moving to SAP S/4HANA.
- **High-Level Solution Design**: Create a high-level solution design that outlines how SAP S/4HANA will fit into the existing IT landscape and what systems will need to be integrated.
- **Project Roadmap**: Develop a preliminary project roadmap that outlines key milestones, timelines, and resource requirements. This roadmap serves as a guide for the rest of the project.

### 14.3.2 Phase 2: Prepare

The **Prepare** phase focuses on building the foundation for the project by setting up the project team, establishing governance structures, and preparing the system environment for the implementation.

Key activities in the Prepare phase include:

- **Project Planning**: Finalize the project plan, including detailed timelines, resource allocation, and budget. The project team is assembled, and roles and responsibilities are defined.
- **System Environment Setup**: Set up the technical infrastructure required for the implementation, including the SAP S/4HANA system landscape (development, testing, and production environments) and any necessary hardware or cloud resources.
- **Kickoff Meeting**: Conduct a project kickoff meeting to align all stakeholders on the project goals, timelines, and deliverables. The kickoff meeting sets the stage for collaboration and ensures that everyone is clear on their roles and responsibilities.

14.3.3 Phase 3: Explore

The **Explore** phase is where the project team begins to define the detailed business requirements and configure SAP S/4HANA based on SAP Best Practices. During this phase, the team works closely with business users to explore the standard functionality of SAP

S/4HANA and determine any customizations or extensions that may be needed.

Key activities in the Explore phase include:

- **Fit-to-Standard Workshops**: Conduct fit-to-standard workshops with business users to compare the organization's business processes with the standard SAP S/4HANA processes. This helps identify gaps and determine whether any customizations or enhancements are required.
- **Detailed Solution Design**: Develop a detailed solution design that outlines how SAP S/4HANA will be configured to meet the organization's business requirements. This includes defining organizational structures, master data, and system parameters.
- **Prototyping**: Build prototypes of key business processes to demonstrate how SAP S/4HANA will work in the organization's environment. Prototyping helps validate the solution design and ensures that it meets business needs.

14.3.4 Phase 4: Realize

The **Realize** phase is where the project team configures and tests the SAP S/4HANA system based on the solution design developed in the Explore phase. This phase includes the configuration of system settings, data migration, and extensive testing to ensure that the system is ready for deployment.

Key activities in the Realize phase include:

- **System Configuration**: Configure SAP S/4HANA based on the solution design and business requirements. This includes setting up organizational structures, defining master data, and configuring key business processes.
- **Data Migration**: Migrate data from legacy systems into SAP S/4HANA. This includes data extraction, cleansing, transformation, and loading, as well as validation to ensure data accuracy.
- **Testing**: Perform extensive testing of the configured system to ensure that it meets the organization's requirements. This includes unit testing, integration testing, and user acceptance testing (UAT). Any issues identified during testing are resolved before moving to the next phase.

14.3.5 Phase 5: Deploy

The **Deploy** phase is the final phase before the SAP S/4HANA system goes live. During this phase, the project team prepares for the system cutover, finalizes training for end-users, and transitions the system to the production environment.

Key activities in the Deploy phase include:

- **Cutover Planning**: Develop a detailed cutover plan that outlines the steps required to transition from the legacy system to SAP S/4HANA. This includes final data migration, system setup, and user access.
- **End-User Training**: Provide comprehensive training for end-users to ensure that they are familiar with the new system and can perform their daily tasks effectively. Training materials and documentation are also finalized during this phase.
- **Go-Live**: Perform the final cutover and go live with SAP S/4HANA. The legacy system is decommissioned, and the SAP S/4HANA system becomes the system of record for business operations.

14.3.6 Phase 6: Run

The **Run** phase focuses on post-go-live activities, including system stabilization, ongoing support, and continuous improvement. During this phase, the project team monitors the system to ensure that it is functioning as expected and addresses any issues that arise.

Key activities in the Run phase include:

- **System Stabilization**: Monitor the performance of the SAP S/4HANA system during the initial stabilization period to ensure that it is running smoothly and that any post-go-live issues are addressed promptly.
- **Ongoing Support**: Provide ongoing support to end-users through a help desk or support team. This includes resolving system issues, answering questions, and providing additional training as needed.
- **Continuous Improvement**: Identify opportunities for continuous improvement in business processes and system functionality. This may include implementing additional features, optimizing system performance, or enhancing reporting and analytics capabilities.

**14.4 Key Benefits of SAP Activate Methodology**

The SAP Activate Methodology offers several key benefits that help organizations successfully implement SAP S/4HANA and other SAP solutions:

14.4.1 Accelerated Implementation

By leveraging SAP Best Practices and Guided Configuration, the SAP Activate Methodology accelerates the implementation process, reducing the time and effort required to configure SAP S/4HANA.

### 14.4.2 Reduced Risk

The structured approach and predefined templates provided by SAP Activate help reduce the risk of errors and delays during the implementation process. The methodology also emphasizes testing and validation at each phase, ensuring that issues are identified and resolved early.

### 14.4.3 Flexibility and Adaptability

SAP Activate is designed to be flexible and adaptable, allowing organizations to customize the methodology to meet their specific needs. Whether the organization is implementing SAP S/4HANA in the cloud, on-premise, or in a hybrid environment, the methodology can be tailored to fit the project's unique requirements.

### 14.4.4 Improved Collaboration

The agile project management approach encourages collaboration between IT, business users, and external consultants. This ensures that business requirements are accurately reflected in the system configuration and that stakeholders are aligned throughout the project.

### 14.4.5 Focus on Continuous Improvement

SAP Activate doesn't stop at go-live. The methodology emphasizes continuous improvement through post-go-live support and ongoing optimization of business processes. This ensures that the organization continues to derive value from SAP S/4HANA long after the initial implementation.

## 14.5 Best Practices for Using SAP Activate Methodology

To get the most out of SAP Activate Methodology, businesses should follow best practices to ensure a successful implementation.

### 14.5.1 Engage Stakeholders Early

Involve key stakeholders from the start of the project to ensure that business requirements are accurately captured and that everyone is aligned on the project goals. This includes involving end-users, department heads, and IT teams in the planning and design phases.

### 14.5.2 Leverage SAP Best Practices

Take full advantage of SAP Best Practices to accelerate the implementation process and ensure that the system is configured based on proven industry standards. Avoid over-customizing the system unless absolutely necessary, as this can increase complexity and cost.

### 14.5.3 Use Agile Principles

Adopt agile principles, such as working in short sprints, delivering incremental value, and seeking continuous feedback. This helps ensure that the project stays on track and that any issues are addressed promptly.

### 14.5.4 Focus on Training and Change Management

Provide comprehensive training and change management to ensure that end-users are comfortable with the new system and can use it effectively. This includes offering training sessions, creating user guides, and providing ongoing support after go-live.

## 14.6 Conclusion: Leveraging SAP Activate for Successful Implementations

The SAP Activate Methodology is a powerful and flexible framework for implementing SAP solutions, including SAP S/4HANA. By combining SAP Best Practices, Guided Configuration, and Agile Project Management, SAP Activate ensures that businesses can implement SAP systems quickly and efficiently while minimizing risk and disruption.

In this chapter, we explored the key components of SAP Activate, the phases of the methodology, and the best practices for using it effectively. By following the SAP Activate Methodology, businesses can achieve a smooth and successful SAP S/4HANA implementation, ensuring that they are well-positioned to drive digital transformation and achieve long-term success.

In the next chapter, we will explore **SAP S/4HANA Cloud and On-Premise Options**.

# Chapter 15: SAP S/4HANA Cloud and On-Premise Options

### 15.1 Introduction to SAP S/4HANA Deployment Options

When implementing **SAP S/4HANA**, businesses can choose between two main deployment options: **SAP S/4HANA Cloud** and **SAP S/4HANA On-Premise**. Both deployment models offer the core capabilities of SAP S/4HANA but differ significantly in terms of infrastructure management, flexibility, scalability, and cost structure. Selecting the right deployment option is crucial for aligning with an organization's IT strategy, budget, and specific business needs.

This chapter will provide a detailed comparison of SAP S/4HANA Cloud and On-Premise options, examining their features, benefits, and key differences. We will explore the hybrid option, which allows businesses to combine the benefits of both models, and provide guidance on how to choose the best deployment model based on organizational requirements.

### 15.2 Overview of SAP S/4HANA Cloud

**SAP S/4HANA Cloud** is a **Software as a Service (SaaS)** version of SAP S/4HANA that runs on SAP's cloud infrastructure. It is designed to provide businesses with the full power of SAP S/4HANA while eliminating the need for on-premise hardware, software maintenance, and manual upgrades. SAP S/4HANA Cloud offers fast implementation, subscription-based pricing, and scalability, making it an attractive option for businesses looking for flexibility and lower upfront costs.

15.2.1 Key Features of SAP S/4HANA Cloud

- **Rapid Deployment**: SAP S/4HANA Cloud can be implemented more quickly than the on-premise version, thanks to its standardized configurations and pre-built integrations. Businesses can go live in a matter of weeks or months, depending on the complexity of the implementation.
- **Automatic Updates**: SAP S/4HANA Cloud is continuously updated by SAP, with new features, enhancements, and security patches automatically deployed. This ensures that businesses always have access to the latest capabilities without the need for manual upgrades or system downtime.
- **Subscription-Based Pricing**: SAP S/4HANA Cloud operates on a subscription-based pricing model, where businesses pay a regular fee based on the number of users and the specific modules they use. This reduces the need for large upfront investments in hardware and software licenses.

- **Scalability and Flexibility**: As a cloud-based solution, SAP S/4HANA Cloud offers scalability, allowing businesses to easily adjust their system capacity as their needs change. This is particularly useful for growing businesses or those with fluctuating workloads.
- **Integrated with SAP Business Technology Platform (BTP)**: SAP S/4HANA Cloud is natively integrated with the **SAP Business Technology Platform (BTP)**, which provides additional services such as data analytics, machine learning, and application development. This allows businesses to extend the functionality of SAP S/4HANA Cloud and innovate on top of the core ERP system.

15.2.2 SAP S/4HANA Cloud Editions

SAP offers multiple editions of SAP S/4HANA Cloud to meet the needs of different businesses:

- **SAP S/4HANA Public Cloud**: This edition is a multi-tenant solution where multiple customers share the same cloud infrastructure and resources. It offers a standardized approach with limited customization options, making it ideal for businesses that prefer a ready-to-use solution with minimal complexity.
- **SAP S/4HANA Private Cloud**: In this edition, each customer has their own dedicated cloud

environment, allowing for more customization and greater control over the system. The private cloud option is suitable for businesses that require more flexibility and want to maintain some level of control over their configurations and processes.

15.2.3 Benefits of SAP S/4HANA Cloud

- **Lower Total Cost of Ownership (TCO)**: By eliminating the need for on-premise infrastructure, SAP S/4HANA Cloud reduces the total cost of ownership. Businesses only pay for the resources they use, and the cloud subscription model spreads costs over time, reducing upfront capital expenditures.
- **Fast Time to Value**: SAP S/4HANA Cloud can be deployed quickly, allowing businesses to start benefiting from the system's capabilities much sooner than with traditional on-premise implementations.
- **Simplified IT Management**: SAP manages the cloud infrastructure, updates, and security, reducing the burden on internal IT teams. This allows businesses to focus on strategic initiatives rather than system maintenance and upgrades.
- **Agility and Innovation**: SAP S/4HANA Cloud is highly scalable, making it easy for businesses to adapt to changing needs. The automatic updates and seamless integration with SAP BTP allow

businesses to continuously innovate and leverage new technologies, such as artificial intelligence (AI) and machine learning (ML).

15.2.4 Limitations of SAP S/4HANA Cloud

- **Limited Customization**: While SAP S/4HANA Cloud offers flexibility, it has more standardized configurations compared to the on-premise version. This may limit the ability to customize certain processes or integrate with highly specialized third-party applications.
- **Data Control and Compliance**: In a cloud environment, data is stored on external servers managed by SAP. For businesses with strict data privacy or compliance requirements (e.g., in the financial or healthcare sectors), this may raise concerns about data security and control.
- **Integration Complexity**: Although SAP S/4HANA Cloud integrates with many other SAP applications, integrating it with legacy systems or non-SAP third-party systems may require additional effort.

**15.3 Overview of SAP S/4HANA On-Premise**

**SAP S/4HANA On-Premise** is a traditional deployment model where the SAP system is installed and managed on the company's own hardware and infrastructure. This model provides maximum control over system configurations, customizations, and data management, making it ideal for businesses with complex requirements or highly specialized processes.

15.3.1 Key Features of SAP S/4HANA On-Premise

- **Full Customization**: SAP S/4HANA On-Premise provides complete flexibility and control over system configurations, allowing businesses to tailor the system to their unique processes and requirements. Custom development and third-party integrations are fully supported, giving businesses the ability to modify and extend the system as needed.
- **Complete Data Control**: With SAP S/4HANA On-Premise, businesses have full control over their data, as it resides within their own data centers. This is particularly important for organizations with stringent data privacy and compliance requirements, such as those in regulated industries.
- **Upgrades Managed by the Business**: Unlike the cloud version, where updates are automatically managed by SAP, businesses running SAP S/4HANA On-Premise have full control over when and how they apply system updates and upgrades. This allows them to manage system changes according to their own schedules and minimize disruptions to business operations.

- **Integration Flexibility**: SAP S/4HANA On-Premise offers more flexibility when it comes to integrating with existing systems, legacy applications, and third-party software. Businesses can design custom interfaces and integrations that meet their specific needs.

### 15.3.2 Benefits of SAP S/4HANA On-Premise

- **Maximum Control**: With SAP S/4HANA On-Premise, businesses have complete control over their system, from infrastructure management to customizations and upgrades. This level of control is essential for organizations with complex IT environments or strict regulatory requirements.
- **Advanced Customization**: The on-premise deployment model supports advanced customizations and modifications, allowing businesses to create highly specialized solutions tailored to their specific processes and needs. This is particularly beneficial for industries with unique workflows or regulatory demands.
- **Data Security and Compliance**: Businesses that require full control over their data and infrastructure can benefit from the on-premise deployment model. This option allows businesses to maintain data within their own data centers and comply with specific security or regulatory requirements.

### 15.3.3 Limitations of SAP S/4HANA On-Premise

- **Higher Initial Costs**: Implementing SAP S/4HANA On-Premise typically involves higher upfront costs, as businesses must invest in hardware, software licenses, and IT resources. In addition, ongoing maintenance, upgrades, and security management increase the total cost of ownership.
- **Longer Deployment Time**: SAP S/4HANA On-Premise implementations tend to take longer compared to the cloud option, as they require more extensive planning, configuration, and system integration. Businesses may face longer project timelines before they can fully realize the benefits of the system.
- **Manual Upgrades**: Unlike SAP S/4HANA Cloud, where upgrades are automatic, businesses running the on-premise version must manage system upgrades themselves. This can be resource-intensive and may require downtime, which could disrupt business operations.

### 15.4 Hybrid Option: SAP S/4HANA Hybrid

For businesses that want to combine the benefits of both cloud and on-premise solutions, SAP offers a **hybrid deployment model**. The hybrid option allows businesses to run specific parts of SAP S/4HANA in the cloud while maintaining other parts on-premise.

### 15.4.1 Key Features of SAP S/4HANA Hybrid

- **Flexibility**: Businesses can choose which processes or systems to run in the cloud and which to maintain on-premise, offering a balance between control, flexibility, and scalability.
- **Cost Optimization**: By running certain workloads in the cloud (e.g., non-critical processes like HR or procurement), businesses can reduce costs while maintaining control over critical or highly customized on-premise systems.
- **Data Security and Compliance**: For businesses that need to keep sensitive data on-premise while leveraging the flexibility of the cloud for other functions, the hybrid model provides the best of both worlds. Organizations can ensure that sensitive data remains within their data centers while still benefiting from cloud scalability.
- **Scalable Innovations**: With the hybrid model, businesses can innovate quickly by deploying new SAP applications in the cloud, such as SAP SuccessFactors or SAP Ariba, while maintaining their core ERP system on-premise.

### 15.4.2 Benefits of SAP S/4HANA Hybrid

- **Tailored Deployment**: Businesses can design a deployment model that fits their specific requirements, leveraging the cloud for speed and cost efficiency, while keeping critical or customized processes on-premise for maximum control.

- **Risk Mitigation**: The hybrid model allows businesses to move non-critical functions to the cloud while reducing the risk associated with fully migrating to the cloud or keeping everything on-premise.
- **Improved Scalability**: By running certain workloads in the cloud, businesses can scale these systems as needed without the constraints of on-premise infrastructure, making it easier to manage fluctuating workloads.

15.4.3 Limitations of SAP S/4HANA Hybrid

- **Complex Integration**: Managing a hybrid environment requires sophisticated integration between cloud and on-premise systems. Ensuring seamless communication between the two environments can increase complexity and require additional resources.
- **Data Governance Challenges**: Businesses must manage data governance carefully to ensure that data is properly synchronized between cloud and on-premise systems. Ensuring data consistency, security, and compliance can be more challenging in a hybrid environment.

## 15.5 Comparing SAP S/4HANA Cloud and On-Premise

The following table summarizes the key differences between SAP S/4HANA Cloud and On-Premise:

| Feature | SAP S/4HANA Cloud | SAP S/4HANA On-Premise |
|---|---|---|
| Deployment Model | SaaS (Subscription-based) | On-premise (License-based) |
| Customization | Limited customization | Full customization |
| Upgrade Management | Automatic upgrades managed by SAP | Manual upgrades managed by the business |
| Implementation Time | Faster (weeks to months) | Longer (months to a year or more) |
| Total Cost of Ownership (TCO) | Lower TCO, especially in the short term | Higher upfront costs, but can be cost-effective long term |
| Control Over Data | Data hosted by SAP in the cloud | Complete control over data (on-premise storage) |
| IT Resource Requirements | Reduced IT resource needs | Higher IT resource requirements |
| Scalability | Easily scalable in the cloud | Limited by on-premise infrastructure |
| Compliance | Requires adherence to SAP's data policies | Complete control over compliance and governance |

### 15.6 Choosing the Right Deployment Option

When deciding between SAP S/4HANA Cloud, On-Premise, or Hybrid deployment models, businesses should consider several factors:

- **Business Size and Growth Plans**: Smaller businesses or rapidly growing organizations may prefer SAP S/4HANA Cloud for its scalability and lower upfront costs, while larger enterprises with complex processes may benefit from the customization options of the On-Premise version.
- **Industry Requirements**: Businesses in regulated industries (e.g., finance, healthcare, manufacturing) may prefer SAP S/4HANA On-Premise for complete control over data security and compliance, while less regulated industries can leverage the cloud for its flexibility.
- **IT Infrastructure and Resources**: Organizations with strong IT teams and infrastructure may choose SAP S/4HANA On-Premise for greater control, while businesses looking to reduce IT overhead might find SAP S/4HANA Cloud more appealing.
- **Customization Needs**: If extensive customization is required, SAP S/4HANA On-Premise provides more flexibility. For businesses that can rely on standard processes and best practices, SAP S/4HANA Cloud offers simplicity and speed.
- **Budget and Cost Considerations**: For businesses looking to minimize upfront capital expenditure, the

subscription-based model of SAP S/4HANA Cloud may be more attractive. However, companies that prefer to invest in long-term infrastructure might opt for SAP S/4HANA On-Premise.

### 15.7 Conclusion: Finding the Right Fit for Your Business

Choosing between **SAP S/4HANA Cloud** and **On-Premise** depends on an organization's needs and goals. SAP S/4HANA Cloud offers flexibility, scalability, and lower upfront costs, ideal for fast innovation and reduced IT management. In contrast, SAP S/4HANA On-Premise provides greater control, customization, and data security, suited for larger enterprises with complex needs.

For businesses seeking the benefits of both models, the **SAP S/4HANA Hybrid** option offers a tailored approach, combining the agility of the cloud with the control of on-premise systems.

In this chapter, we explored the features, benefits, and limitations of each deployment model and provided guidance on how to choose the best option for your organization.

In the next chapter, we will explore **Best Practices for SAP S/4HANA Security** in detail.

# Chapter 16: Best Practices for SAP S/4HANA Security

## 16.1 Introduction to SAP S/4HANA Security

As businesses increasingly rely on SAP S/4HANA for critical operations such as finance, supply chain management, and human resources, ensuring the security of the system and the data it processes becomes essential. SAP S/4HANA, whether deployed in the cloud or on-premise, holds vast amounts of sensitive data, making it a potential target for cyberattacks, data breaches, and internal misuse. A robust security framework is necessary to protect the integrity, confidentiality, and availability of data, ensuring that business operations remain secure and compliant with industry standards and regulations.

This chapter will outline the key security features of SAP S/4HANA and provide best practices for managing security in areas such as user access, data protection, system configuration, and compliance. Whether your organization is implementing SAP S/4HANA Cloud, On-Premise, or a hybrid deployment, these practices will help safeguard your ERP environment and mitigate potential risks.

## 16.2 SAP S/4HANA Security Architecture

SAP S/4HANA's security architecture is designed to protect business data and applications from unauthorized access, data breaches, and malicious activities. The security model in SAP S/4HANA encompasses several layers of protection, including user authentication, authorization management, data encryption, and system monitoring.

16.2.1 Identity and Access Management (IAM)

Identity and Access Management (IAM) is a core component of SAP S/4HANA's security architecture. It ensures that only authorized users can access the system and perform specific tasks based on their roles and responsibilities. IAM encompasses user authentication, role-based access control (RBAC), and identity provisioning.

Key features of SAP S/4HANA IAM include:

- **User Authentication**: SAP S/4HANA supports various methods of authentication, including **Single Sign-On (SSO)**, SAP password policies, and multi-factor authentication (MFA). These measures verify the identity of users before granting access to the system.
- **Role-Based Access Control (RBAC)**: SAP S/4HANA follows a role-based access control

model, where access to system resources is granted based on predefined roles. Users are assigned roles that specify their permissions, ensuring that they can only access the data and functions required for their job.

- **Identity Provisioning**: SAP S/4HANA integrates with external identity management systems, allowing businesses to automate the provisioning and deprovisioning of user accounts across multiple applications. This integration ensures that user access is efficiently managed, reducing the risk of unauthorized access.

16.2.2 Data Encryption and Protection

Data security is a critical concern for organizations using SAP S/4HANA, especially in cloud environments where data may be stored externally. SAP S/4HANA provides several data protection mechanisms to safeguard sensitive information.

Key data protection features include:

- **Data Encryption**: SAP S/4HANA supports data encryption both at rest and in transit. Data at rest (stored in databases or files) is encrypted using strong encryption algorithms, while data in transit (moving between systems or users) is protected using **Transport Layer Security (TLS)** to prevent interception.

- **Data Masking and Anonymization**: To protect sensitive data from unauthorized users, SAP S/4HANA allows organizations to implement data masking and anonymization. This ensures that confidential data, such as customer information or financial records, is not exposed to users who do not have the appropriate permissions.
- **Data Access Logging**: SAP S/4HANA enables organizations to log and monitor access to sensitive data, providing a trail of user actions that can be reviewed in the event of a security incident or audit.

16.2.3 System Monitoring and Threat Detection

System monitoring and threat detection are essential for maintaining the security of SAP S/4HANA environments. SAP provides several tools and features to help organizations detect suspicious activities and respond to potential threats in real time.

Key system monitoring features include:

- **SAP EarlyWatch Alert**: This service monitors the health of SAP systems and provides alerts for potential performance, configuration, or security issues. It helps organizations proactively address vulnerabilities before they are exploited.

- **SAP Security Audit Log**: SAP S/4HANA includes a security audit log that records key security-related events, such as failed login attempts, changes to user roles, and modifications to system configurations. This log can be analyzed to detect abnormal patterns and potential security threats.
- **Threat Detection with SAP Enterprise Threat Detection (ETD)**: SAP ETD is an advanced tool that helps organizations identify and respond to security threats in real time. It uses machine learning and pattern recognition to analyze log data and detect anomalies that may indicate a security breach.

**16.3 Best Practices for SAP S/4HANA Security**

To ensure the security of SAP S/4HANA, businesses must adopt best practices across several key areas, including access control, data protection, configuration management, and compliance. The following sections outline these best practices in detail.

16.3.1 User Access Management

User access management is one of the most critical aspects of SAP S/4HANA security. It ensures that users can only access the data and functions necessary for their roles, reducing the risk of unauthorized access and data breaches.

**Best Practices for User Access Management**:

- **Implement Role-Based Access Control (RBAC)**: Ensure that user access is based on predefined roles aligned with their job responsibilities. Each role should have the minimum required permissions to perform tasks (known as the principle of least privilege).
- **Use Segregation of Duties (SoD)**: Implement segregation of duties to prevent conflicts of interest, such as having the same user responsible for both creating and approving transactions. SoD reduces the risk of fraud and errors by ensuring that critical business processes require oversight from multiple individuals.
- **Enable Multi-Factor Authentication (MFA)**: Require multi-factor authentication for access to critical functions and sensitive data. MFA adds an extra layer of security by requiring users to provide two or more forms of verification before gaining access.
- **Regularly Review User Roles and Access**: Conduct periodic reviews of user roles and access rights to ensure that users do not have unnecessary or excessive permissions. This is particularly important when employees change roles or leave the organization.

16.3.2 Data Security and Encryption

Protecting data within SAP S/4HANA is essential for ensuring its confidentiality, integrity, and availability. Businesses must implement encryption and data protection strategies to safeguard sensitive information.

**Best Practices for Data Security:**

- **Encrypt Data at Rest and in Transit**: Use strong encryption algorithms to encrypt data stored in databases, file systems, and backups (data at rest). Ensure that all data transmitted between systems, applications, and users is encrypted using TLS or similar encryption protocols (data in transit).
- **Implement Data Masking for Sensitive Information**: Use data masking to hide sensitive information (e.g., Social Security numbers, credit card details) from users who do not require access to the full data. Masking can be applied to fields in reports or transactions to protect sensitive data.
- **Apply Data Anonymization for Analytics**: For businesses that use SAP S/4HANA for analytics, anonymizing sensitive data before it is analyzed or shared can help maintain privacy while still allowing valuable insights to be extracted from the data.

- **Monitor Data Access**: Enable data access logging and monitoring to track who is accessing sensitive data. Regularly review access logs to detect any suspicious behavior or unauthorized access attempts.

16.3.3 System Configuration and Hardening

System configuration and hardening involve securing the underlying infrastructure and ensuring that all configurations are aligned with security best practices. Proper configuration reduces the risk of vulnerabilities and exploits.

**Best Practices for System Configuration and Hardening**:

- **Follow SAP Security Notes**: SAP regularly releases security notes that provide guidance on addressing vulnerabilities and system updates. Organizations should ensure that they apply relevant security notes promptly to patch vulnerabilities in their SAP S/4HANA environment.
- **Disable Unused Services and Ports**: Disable any unnecessary services, ports, or protocols that are not being used. This reduces the attack surface of the SAP S/4HANA system and prevents potential exploits.
- **Use Secure Communication Protocols**: Ensure that all communication between systems and

applications uses secure protocols, such as HTTPS or TLS, to protect data from being intercepted during transmission.
- **Regularly Audit and Monitor System Settings**: Conduct regular audits of system configurations, security policies, and user access rights to ensure that the system is properly secured and that no unauthorized changes have been made.

16.3.4 Patch Management and Software Updates

Keeping SAP S/4HANA up to date with the latest patches and software updates is critical for protecting against vulnerabilities and security threats.

**Best Practices for Patch Management**:

- **Apply Patches Promptly**: Implement a patch management process that ensures critical patches are applied as soon as they are released. Delaying patches can leave the system exposed to known vulnerabilities.
- **Test Patches in a Sandbox Environment**: Before applying patches to the production system, test them in a sandbox or quality assurance environment to ensure that they do not introduce compatibility issues or affect system performance.
- **Automate Patch Deployment (Cloud Environments)**: For businesses using SAP

S/4HANA Cloud, take advantage of automated updates and patches provided by SAP. Cloud environments typically receive patches automatically, reducing the risk of manual errors or delayed updates.

16.3.5 Compliance and Auditing

Maintaining compliance with industry standards, regulations, and internal policies is a key aspect of SAP S/4HANA security. Businesses must implement security controls that ensure compliance with laws such as the **General Data Protection Regulation (GDPR), Health Insurance Portability and Accountability Act (HIPAA),** and **Sarbanes-Oxley Act (SOX).**

**Best Practices for Compliance and Auditing:**

- **Implement Access Controls for Sensitive Data**: Ensure that access to sensitive data, such as financial records or personally identifiable information (PII), is restricted to authorized users only. Document the controls in place to comply with data protection regulations like GDPR.
- **Enable Audit Logging**: Use SAP's audit logging features to track system activity, including changes to user roles, system configurations, and access to sensitive data. Regularly review

these logs to detect unauthorized activity or compliance violations.

- **Conduct Regular Security Audits**: Perform regular security audits to assess the effectiveness of security controls, identify gaps, and ensure compliance with regulatory requirements. Use third-party auditors if necessary to provide an unbiased assessment.
- **Maintain Audit Trails**: Ensure that all changes to system configurations, business processes, and access rights are recorded in an audit trail. This helps demonstrate compliance during external audits and provides accountability for system changes.

## 16.4 Monitoring and Incident Response in SAP S/4HANA

Continuous monitoring and a well-defined incident response plan are essential for maintaining the security of SAP S/4HANA environments. Proactive monitoring helps detect potential threats before they escalate, while a structured incident response plan ensures that security incidents are managed effectively.

**Best Practices for Monitoring and Incident Response:**

- **Implement Real-Time Monitoring**: Use SAP tools like **SAP EarlyWatch Alert** and **SAP Enterprise Threat Detection** to monitor system performance and detect security threats in real time. Set up alerts for critical events, such as failed login attempts, unauthorized access, or abnormal system behavior.

- **Develop an Incident Response Plan**: Create a comprehensive incident response plan that outlines the steps to take in the event of a security breach or cyberattack. The plan should include roles and responsibilities, communication protocols, and procedures for containing and mitigating threats.
- **Perform Regular Security Drills**: Conduct security drills and simulations to test the effectiveness of the incident response plan. These exercises help ensure that the response team is prepared to act quickly and efficiently during a real security incident.
- **Document and Analyze Incidents**: After a security incident, document the details of the incident, including how it occurred, how it was resolved, and any lessons learned. Use this information to improve security measures and prevent similar incidents in the future.

### 16.5 Conclusion: Securing SAP S/4HANA for the Future

Securing SAP S/4HANA is a critical responsibility for businesses that rely on the system to manage their operations and process sensitive data. By following best practices in areas such as access control, data encryption, system configuration, and compliance, organizations can reduce the risk of cyberattacks, data breaches, and internal threats.

In this chapter, we explored the key components of SAP S/4HANA's security architecture and provided detailed guidance on how to implement robust security measures. Whether deployed in the cloud or on-premise, SAP S/4HANA must be secured using a comprehensive, multi-layered approach that includes monitoring, auditing, and incident response.

In the next chapter, we will explore **Developing Custom Applications in SAP S/4HANA** in detail.

# Chapter 17: Developing Custom Applications in SAP S/4HANA

### 17.1 Introduction to Custom Application Development in SAP S/4HANA

SAP S/4HANA is a robust, integrated enterprise resource planning (ERP) system designed to support standard business processes across industries. However, many organizations have unique requirements that go beyond the out-of-the-box capabilities provided by SAP S/4HANA. To meet these needs, businesses can develop **custom applications** that extend or enhance the functionality of the core SAP S/4HANA system.

Developing custom applications in SAP S/4HANA allows organizations to tailor their ERP system to specific workflows, integrate with third-party systems, and provide specialized functionality to meet business requirements. Custom applications can be developed using SAP's modern development platforms, such as **SAP Business Technology Platform (BTP)** and **SAP Fiori**, leveraging technologies like **ABAP**, **SAPUI5**, and **OData services**.

This chapter will explore the tools, technologies, and best practices for developing custom applications in SAP S/4HANA. We will cover the various approaches for building applications in both **on-premise** and **cloud**

**environments**, and how organizations can integrate these applications seamlessly with SAP S/4HANA.

## 17.2 Key Technologies for Custom Development in SAP S/4HANA

Developing custom applications in SAP S/4HANA requires familiarity with a range of technologies and tools that are part of the SAP development ecosystem. Understanding these technologies helps organizations choose the right approach for building custom functionality.

### 17.2.1 ABAP (Advanced Business Application Programming)

**ABAP** (Advanced Business Application Programming) is SAP's proprietary programming language and is widely used for developing custom applications and enhancements within SAP S/4HANA. ABAP is primarily used for backend logic, data processing, and integrating custom applications with SAP's core modules.

Key features of ABAP for custom development include:

- **Core Data Services (CDS)**: ABAP CDS is used to create views and models for data access in SAP S/4HANA. CDS views enable real-time access to transactional data and serve as a foundation for building custom applications that interact with the underlying database.

- **ABAP Managed Services (AMS)**: ABAP Managed Services offer developers tools for building and running custom applications in both on-premise and cloud environments. AMS ensures that custom code adheres to SAP's best practices and performance standards.
- **Extensibility**: ABAP provides various extensibility options, including user exits, Business Add-Ins (BAdIs), and enhancement spots, allowing developers to extend SAP S/4HANA without modifying the standard codebase.

17.2.2 SAP Fiori and SAPUI5

**SAP Fiori** is SAP's user experience (UX) platform that provides a modern, responsive interface for interacting with SAP applications. **SAPUI5** is the underlying technology used to build SAP Fiori applications. It is based on HTML5, JavaScript, and CSS, enabling developers to create custom, web-based applications that integrate with SAP S/4HANA.

Key features of SAP Fiori and SAPUI5 include:

- **Responsive Design**: SAP Fiori applications are designed to work across devices, including desktops, tablets, and smartphones. This ensures that users can access custom applications from anywhere, enhancing mobility and productivity.

- **Custom Fiori Apps**: Developers can create custom Fiori apps using SAPUI5 and integrate them seamlessly with SAP S/4HANA. These apps provide a personalized user experience, tailored to specific roles or business processes.
- **OData Integration**: SAP Fiori apps interact with SAP S/4HANA data using **OData services**, which provide a standard protocol for querying and updating data over the web. This allows Fiori apps to read and write data from SAP S/4HANA in real-time.

17.2.3 SAP Business Technology Platform (BTP)

**SAP Business Technology Platform (BTP)** provides a cloud-based environment for developing, running, and managing custom applications that integrate with SAP S/4HANA. BTP supports a variety of development tools and services, including ABAP, SAP Fiori, and third-party languages, enabling developers to build applications in both **cloud** and **hybrid environments**.

Key features of SAP BTP include:

- **Application Development**: BTP supports the development of custom applications using a range of programming languages, such as **ABAP**, **Java**, **Node.js**, and **Python**. This flexibility allows developers to build applications based on their preferred technologies.

- **Integration Services**: SAP BTP includes **SAP Integration Suite**, which provides pre-built connectors, APIs, and integration tools to connect custom applications with SAP S/4HANA and other systems.
- **SAP HANA Database Services**: SAP BTP includes access to the **SAP HANA Cloud** database, enabling developers to build data-driven applications that leverage the real-time processing capabilities of SAP HANA.
- **Extensibility**: With BTP, developers can extend SAP S/4HANA by building side-by-side extensions that run in the cloud. These extensions allow businesses to innovate without altering the core SAP S/4HANA codebase, reducing the risk of disruptions during upgrades.

## 17.3 Types of Custom Applications in SAP S/4HANA

Custom applications in SAP S/4HANA can be developed to address a variety of use cases, from enhancing existing business processes to creating entirely new functionality. Below are common types of custom applications that businesses may develop.

### 17.3.1 User Interfaces and Dashboards

Many businesses require custom **user interfaces** or **dashboards** to provide a tailored view of key data and insights. SAP Fiori and SAPUI5 are typically used to create these interfaces, offering a modern and intuitive user experience.

Examples of custom UI applications include:

- **Executive Dashboards**: Custom dashboards that provide real-time visibility into key performance indicators (KPIs) such as sales revenue, inventory levels, and financial performance.
- **Role-Specific Applications**: Applications designed for specific user roles, such as purchasing managers or HR administrators, that streamline workflows and provide a personalized experience.

### 17.3.2 Custom Reports and Analytics

Businesses often need custom reports that go beyond the standard reporting capabilities of SAP S/4HANA. Developers can create custom reports using ABAP or SAP HANA to process and analyze large volumes of data.

Examples of custom reporting applications include:

- **Financial Reports**: Custom financial reports that aggregate data from multiple sources to provide insights into profitability, cost analysis, and cash flow.
- **Sales Analytics**: Custom sales analytics applications that track performance metrics such as conversion rates, customer acquisition, and order fulfillment.

17.3.3 Workflow Automation

Custom applications can automate complex workflows, reducing manual effort and increasing operational efficiency. SAP S/4HANA's **workflow engine** can be customized to create new approval processes, task assignments, and automated notifications.

Examples of custom workflow applications include:

- **Purchase Order Approvals**: A custom workflow that automates the approval process for purchase orders, ensuring that requests are routed to the appropriate managers for review and approval.
- **Leave Request Automation**: An HR application that automates the submission and approval of employee leave requests, integrating with time and attendance systems.

17.3.4 Data Entry and Processing Applications

Many organizations require custom data entry applications to streamline data input and processing. These applications are often built using Fiori and ABAP and integrate directly with the SAP S/4HANA backend.

Examples of data entry applications include:

- **Material Master Data Entry**: A custom application that simplifies the process of entering and maintaining material master data, ensuring data consistency and reducing errors.
- **Sales Order Processing**: A sales order entry application that allows sales representatives to create and manage customer orders from any device, with real-time validation and integration with the SAP S/4HANA backend.

## 17.4 Best Practices for Custom Application Development in SAP S/4HANA

Developing custom applications for SAP S/4HANA requires careful planning, adherence to best practices, and the use of SAP's recommended development tools and frameworks. Below are best practices that organizations should follow to ensure successful custom development.

17.4.1 Leverage SAP's Extensibility Frameworks

SAP provides several extensibility frameworks that allow businesses to customize their SAP S/4HANA environment without modifying the core system. Using these frameworks reduces the risk of issues during system upgrades and ensures that custom code adheres to SAP's best practices.

Key extensibility frameworks include:

- **In-App Extensibility**: In-app extensibility allows businesses to customize SAP S/4HANA directly through the Fiori interface. This includes making changes to UI elements, adding fields, and modifying business logic using **custom fields** and **custom logic**.
- **Side-by-Side Extensibility**: For more complex customizations, side-by-side extensibility allows developers to build extensions on **SAP BTP** that interact with SAP S/4HANA via APIs and OData services. This approach ensures that custom applications remain separate from the core system, reducing the risk of disruption during upgrades.

17.4.2 Follow SAP's Development Guidelines

SAP provides detailed development guidelines and best practices for building custom applications, including

213

naming conventions, coding standards, and performance optimization techniques. Following these guidelines ensures that custom applications are secure, scalable, and maintainable.

Key guidelines include:

- **Use ABAP Development Guidelines**: Developers building custom ABAP applications should follow SAP's ABAP development guidelines, which cover topics such as code structure, performance optimization, and error handling.
- **Leverage SAPUI5 Design Principles**: When building Fiori applications, follow SAP's **SAP Fiori Design Guidelines** to ensure that the custom application aligns with the Fiori design language and provides a consistent user experience.

17.4.3 Ensure Secure Development Practices

Security is a critical consideration in custom application development. Custom applications that access sensitive data or integrate with external systems must be designed with security in mind.

Best practices for secure development include:

- **Use OAuth for Authentication**: When building custom applications that interact with SAP

S/4HANA via APIs, use **OAuth** for secure authentication and access control.

- **Implement Role-Based Authorization**: Ensure that custom applications adhere to role-based authorization controls, limiting access to sensitive data and functions based on user roles.
- **Regularly Test for Vulnerabilities**: Conduct regular security testing, including **penetration testing** and **code reviews**, to identify and fix vulnerabilities in custom applications.

17.4.4 Optimize Performance

Custom applications that interact with large datasets or involve complex calculations can impact the performance of SAP S/4HANA if not properly optimized.

Best practices for performance optimization include:

- **Use CDS Views for Data Access**: When accessing data from SAP S/4HANA, use **Core Data Services (CDS) views** to retrieve data efficiently. CDS views are optimized for performance and allow real-time access to transactional data.
- **Minimize Round-Trips to the Backend**: Reduce the number of round-trips between the custom application and the SAP S/4HANA backend by batching requests and minimizing calls to the server.

- **Monitor Performance Metrics**: Use SAP's performance monitoring tools to track the performance of custom applications and identify areas where optimization is needed.

17.4.5 Plan for Maintenance and Upgrades

Custom applications must be designed to accommodate future system upgrades and changes to the SAP S/4HANA environment. Businesses should plan for the long-term maintenance of custom code, including regular updates and testing.

Best practices for maintenance include:

- **Use Version Control**: Implement version control for all custom code, ensuring that changes can be tracked and rolled back if necessary.
- **Test Custom Code After Upgrades**: When upgrading SAP S/4HANA, thoroughly test all custom applications to ensure compatibility and resolve any issues introduced by new system features.
- **Document Customizations**: Maintain detailed documentation of all custom applications, including their purpose, functionality, and integration points with SAP S/4HANA.

## 17.5 Conclusion: Unlocking Business Value with Custom Applications in SAP S/4HANA

Custom applications in SAP S/4HANA allow businesses to extend the functionality of their ERP system, tailor processes to specific needs, and integrate with third-party systems. By leveraging SAP's development platforms, such as ABAP, SAP Fiori, and SAP Business Technology Platform, businesses can create powerful, scalable applications that enhance the capabilities of SAP S/4HANA.

In this chapter, we explored the key technologies and best practices for custom development in SAP S/4HANA. By following SAP's development guidelines, optimizing performance, and ensuring security, businesses can create custom applications that deliver long-term value while maintaining the integrity of the core ERP system.

In next chapter, we will explore **SAP S/4HANA for in the context of Business Users**.

# Chapter 18: SAP S/4HANA for Business Users

## 18.1 Introduction to SAP S/4HANA for Business Users

SAP S/4HANA is a comprehensive enterprise resource planning (ERP) system designed to streamline core business processes across industries. While it is a powerful tool for IT and technical teams, it also plays a critical role in empowering **business users**—those who rely on the system to execute daily tasks such as managing sales, finance, procurement, production, and human resources.

SAP S/4HANA is designed to be user-friendly, intuitive, and responsive, offering a modern user interface (UI) through **SAP Fiori**. Business users can interact with the system in a way that aligns with their roles, making it easier to access information, make decisions, and complete tasks efficiently.

This chapter will explore how SAP S/4HANA is used by business users across different functions, the key features that enhance user productivity, and best practices for maximizing the system's potential in day-to-day operations.

## 18.2 The Role of Business Users in SAP S/4HANA

Business users are integral to the daily operation of SAP S/4HANA. They are the individuals who interact with the system to perform essential functions, such as creating sales orders, managing inventory, processing invoices, and running financial reports. SAP S/4HANA's architecture supports a variety of business users, each with specific roles and responsibilities.

### 18.2.1 Key Roles of Business Users in SAP S/4HANA

- **Sales Managers and Representatives**: Sales teams use SAP S/4HANA to manage customer interactions, track orders, monitor inventory, and generate sales forecasts. They rely on the system to ensure timely order fulfillment and enhance customer service.
- **Procurement Officers**: Procurement teams use SAP S/4HANA to manage supplier relationships, create purchase orders, monitor deliveries, and track spend. The system helps procurement professionals ensure that materials and services are purchased at the best price and delivered on time.
- **Financial Controllers and Accountants**: Finance teams leverage SAP S/4HANA to manage financial transactions, create financial reports, reconcile accounts, and ensure compliance with accounting standards. Financial users rely on

real-time data for decision-making and reporting.

- **Production Managers**: In manufacturing environments, production managers use SAP S/4HANA to schedule production runs, track inventory levels, and monitor equipment performance. The system helps ensure that production processes are optimized and that products are delivered on schedule.
- **Human Resource Managers**: HR teams use SAP S/4HANA to manage employee data, payroll, benefits, and time tracking. The system allows HR professionals to streamline recruitment, onboarding, and employee management processes.

**18.3 The SAP Fiori User Experience for Business Users**

A significant advancement in SAP S/4HANA is the **SAP Fiori** user interface. SAP Fiori provides a simple, role-based, and responsive experience that is designed to help business users complete tasks more efficiently.

18.3.1 Key Features of SAP Fiori for Business Users

- **Role-Based Dashboards**: SAP Fiori offers role-specific homepages and dashboards, providing business users with quick access to the tasks and data they need. For example, a procurement officer's dashboard may display open purchase orders, pending approvals, and supplier performance metrics, while a sales manager's dashboard might focus on order status, sales performance, and customer inquiries.

- **Personalized User Experience**: Business users can customize their Fiori launchpad by adding or removing tiles, setting up favorites, and arranging their dashboards to match their daily workflows. This personalization helps users focus on the most relevant tasks and data.
- **Responsive Design**: SAP Fiori applications are designed to be responsive, meaning they work seamlessly across different devices, including desktops, tablets, and smartphones. This allows business users to access the system from anywhere and at any time, improving mobility and flexibility.
- **Notifications and Alerts**: SAP Fiori provides real-time notifications and alerts to keep business users informed of critical events, such as approval requests, stock shortages, or pending invoices. These alerts enable users to take immediate action, ensuring that business processes are not delayed.
- **Embedded Analytics**: SAP Fiori integrates with SAP S/4HANA's analytics capabilities, allowing users to generate reports and visualize key data directly from their dashboards. This real-time insight enables users to make informed decisions quickly.

18.3.2 Common SAP Fiori Applications for Business Users

SAP Fiori provides a wide range of pre-built applications that cater to the needs of different business users. Below are examples of common SAP Fiori apps used in various roles:

- **Create Sales Order**: This app allows sales representatives to create and manage customer orders, check product availability, and track delivery status. It simplifies the order management process by providing a guided workflow for entering customer details and order information.
- **Approve Purchase Orders**: Procurement managers can use this app to review, approve, or reject purchase orders directly from their mobile device or desktop. This helps streamline the approval process and ensure that orders are processed without delays.
- **Manage Payments**: Financial controllers can use this app to monitor outgoing payments, process invoices, and ensure that vendors are paid on time. The app provides visibility into payment terms, due dates, and cash flow management.
- **Track Production Orders**: Production managers can use this app to track the progress of production orders, monitor inventory levels, and manage production schedules. It provides real-

time insights into the status of production runs and potential bottlenecks.

- **My Timesheet**: HR professionals and employees can use this app to track and submit working hours, leave requests, and project assignments. It simplifies time management and ensures accurate payroll processing.

### 18.4 Key Functional Areas in SAP S/4HANA for Business Users

SAP S/4HANA covers a wide range of functional areas, each supporting the specific needs of different departments and business processes. Below, we explore the key modules used by business users in SAP S/4HANA.

18.4.1 Sales and Distribution (SD)

The **Sales and Distribution (SD)** module in SAP S/4HANA is used by sales teams to manage the entire order-to-cash process. Business users rely on SD to create and process sales orders, manage customer data, and monitor inventory levels to fulfill orders.

Key tasks for business users in SD include:

- **Sales Order Processing**: Business users create and manage sales orders, ensuring that customer requests are fulfilled accurately and on time.

- **Pricing and Discounts**: Users manage pricing conditions, including special promotions, discounts, and volume pricing, to optimize sales margins.
- **Shipping and Delivery**: Sales and logistics teams use SD to coordinate shipping, track deliveries, and manage returns, ensuring smooth order fulfillment.

18.4.2 Materials Management (MM)

The **Materials Management (MM)** module is essential for procurement teams and inventory managers, helping them track materials, manage suppliers, and ensure that production processes have the necessary inputs.

Key tasks for business users in MM include:

- **Purchase Requisition and Orders**: Procurement teams create purchase requisitions and orders, ensuring that materials and services are sourced at the right time and at the best price.
- **Inventory Management**: Inventory managers track stock levels, manage goods receipts, and ensure that materials are available for production or sales.

- **Supplier Evaluation**: Users can assess supplier performance based on criteria such as delivery times, quality, and price to optimize procurement decisions.

18.4.3 Financial Accounting (FI)

The **Financial Accounting (FI)** module is used by finance teams to manage all aspects of financial reporting, including accounts payable, accounts receivable, and general ledger management.

Key tasks for business users in FI include:

- **Accounts Payable and Receivable**: Finance users track vendor invoices, process payments, and manage customer payments to ensure that cash flow is maintained.
- **Financial Reporting**: Financial controllers generate reports such as balance sheets, income statements, and cash flow statements, providing real-time insights into the financial health of the organization.
- **Asset Accounting**: Users manage the lifecycle of company assets, including acquisition, depreciation, and disposal, ensuring accurate financial records.

18.4.4 Production Planning (PP)

The **Production Planning (PP)** module is used by production managers to plan and monitor manufacturing processes, ensuring that production schedules are met and resources are optimized.

Key tasks for business users in PP include:

- **Production Scheduling**: Production managers create production plans and schedules, ensuring that products are manufactured on time and that resources are allocated efficiently.
- **Bill of Materials (BOM) Management**: Users manage BOMs, which list the components needed to manufacture a product, ensuring that the correct materials are available for production.
- **Capacity Planning**: PP allows production managers to assess capacity utilization and make adjustments to ensure that production processes are not delayed.

18.4.5 Human Capital Management (HCM)

The **Human Capital Management (HCM)** module is used by HR teams to manage employee data, payroll, time tracking, and performance management. Business users in HR rely on HCM to streamline HR processes and ensure compliance with labor regulations.

Key tasks for business users in HCM include:

- **Employee Master Data Management**: HR professionals manage employee records, including personal information, job assignments, and benefits enrollment.
- **Payroll Processing**: Payroll teams use HCM to calculate wages, process payroll runs, and ensure compliance with tax regulations.
- **Time and Attendance Management**: HR professionals track employee attendance, manage leave requests, and ensure that working hours are accurately recorded.

## 18.5 Best Practices for Business Users in SAP S/4HANA

To maximize the value of SAP S/4HANA, business users should follow best practices that improve efficiency, accuracy, and collaboration.

### 18.5.1 Utilize Role-Specific Dashboards

Business users should customize their SAP Fiori dashboards to display the most relevant tasks, reports, and notifications based on their role. This personalization ensures that users can access the information they need quickly and avoid distractions.

### 18.5.2 Leverage Embedded Analytics

SAP S/4HANA's embedded analytics provide business users with real-time insights into key metrics, such as sales performance, inventory levels, and financial health. Users should regularly review these analytics to make informed decisions and identify trends that may require action.

### 18.5.3 Automate Routine Tasks

Business users can automate routine tasks using SAP S/4HANA's workflow and automation features. For example, automating purchase order approvals or invoice processing can reduce manual effort and improve efficiency.

### 18.5.4 Collaborate Across Teams

SAP S/4HANA is an integrated platform, meaning that data from one department can impact others. Business users should collaborate with colleagues in other departments (e.g., finance, sales, procurement) to ensure that processes are aligned and that data is shared effectively.

### 18.5.5 Keep Up with System Updates and Enhancements

SAP regularly releases updates and new features for SAP S/4HANA. Business users should stay informed about these updates and work with their IT teams to adopt new capabilities that can improve productivity and streamline workflows.

### 18.6 Conclusion: Empowering Business Users with SAP S/4HANA

SAP S/4HANA provides business users with the tools and insights they need to perform their daily tasks efficiently, from managing sales orders and processing financial transactions to optimizing production and managing HR processes. By leveraging the SAP Fiori interface, embedded analytics, and role-based dashboards, business users can gain real-time visibility into critical data and improve decision-making.

In this chapter, we explored how SAP S/4HANA supports business roles, key modules for users, and best practices. By adopting these, business users can unlock the full potential of SAP S/4HANA and contribute to their organization's success.

In the next chapter, we will dive into **Future Trends and Innovations in SAP S/4HANA**.

# Chapter 19: Future Trends and Innovations in SAP S/4HANA

### 19.1 Introduction to Future Trends in SAP S/4HANA

As technology continues to evolve, **SAP S/4HANA** is at the forefront of innovation in enterprise resource planning (ERP) systems. Since its launch, SAP S/4HANA has transformed how businesses operate by leveraging the power of in-memory computing, real-time data processing, and a modern user experience. As organizations increasingly adopt digital transformation strategies, the future of SAP S/4HANA will focus on further enhancing automation, integrating emerging technologies, and delivering new business models.

In this chapter, we will explore the future trends and innovations in SAP S/4HANA that are poised to shape the next generation of ERP systems. From artificial intelligence (AI) and machine learning (ML) to the Internet of Things (IoT) and blockchain, we will examine how SAP S/4HANA is evolving to meet the challenges and opportunities of the digital age.

### 19.2 Artificial Intelligence and Machine Learning in SAP S/4HANA

Artificial Intelligence (AI) and Machine Learning (ML) are among the most significant trends impacting enterprise software, and SAP S/4HANA is embracing these technologies to enable smarter, more efficient operations. AI and ML can be integrated into various SAP S/4HANA processes to enhance decision-making, automate routine tasks, and deliver predictive insights.

19.2.1 AI-Driven Automation

One of the primary benefits of AI in SAP S/4HANA is the ability to automate repetitive tasks, reducing manual effort and minimizing human error. For example, AI-driven automation can streamline processes such as invoice processing, purchase order approvals, and financial reconciliations by intelligently identifying patterns and making recommendations.

Key applications of AI-driven automation include:

- **Automated Invoice Matching**: Using AI, SAP S/4HANA can automatically match invoices to purchase orders and goods receipts, significantly reducing the time finance teams spend on invoice processing.
- **Smart Procurement**: AI can analyze procurement data to identify optimal suppliers, predict potential delays, and recommend purchase orders based on historical data, reducing procurement cycle times and improving supplier relationships.

19.2.2 Machine Learning for Predictive Analytics

Machine Learning models within SAP S/4HANA allow businesses to leverage predictive analytics, providing insights into future trends, potential risks, and opportunities. By analyzing historical data and recognizing patterns, ML can deliver predictive insights that drive proactive decision-making.

Key use cases of predictive analytics in SAP S/4HANA include:

- **Demand Forecasting**: ML algorithms can analyze sales data and external market trends to predict future product demand, enabling businesses to optimize production schedules and inventory levels.
- **Predictive Maintenance**: In manufacturing environments, ML can predict equipment failures by analyzing sensor data from machinery. This enables businesses to perform maintenance proactively, reducing downtime and extending the life of critical assets.
- **Cash Flow Forecasting**: ML models can predict future cash flows by analyzing financial transactions, payment histories, and external economic factors, allowing businesses to manage liquidity more effectively.

### 19.2.3 Intelligent Insights with SAP Leonardo

SAP has integrated AI and ML capabilities into the **SAP Leonardo** innovation portfolio, which complements SAP S/4HANA by enabling businesses to develop intelligent applications that automate processes and generate real-time insights. SAP Leonardo's AI and ML services can be used to build custom solutions that extend the capabilities of SAP S/4HANA.

## 19.3 The Internet of Things (IoT) and SAP S/4HANA

The **Internet of Things (IoT)** is revolutionizing industries by connecting physical devices to digital systems, enabling businesses to capture and analyze real-time data from sensors, machines, and other IoT-enabled devices. SAP S/4HANA's integration with IoT opens up new opportunities for businesses to optimize operations, enhance product innovation, and improve customer experiences.

### 19.3.1 IoT-Enabled Supply Chain Management

SAP S/4HANA is leveraging IoT to create intelligent supply chains where real-time data from sensors and devices can be used to track inventory, monitor shipments, and ensure product quality. This level of visibility allows businesses to respond faster to supply chain disruptions, optimize logistics, and improve demand planning.

Key use cases of IoT in supply chain management include:

- **Real-Time Inventory Tracking**: IoT sensors can track the location and condition of goods as they move through the supply chain. By integrating this data with SAP S/4HANA, businesses can monitor inventory levels in real time and make adjustments to procurement or production as needed.
- **Cold Chain Management**: In industries such as pharmaceuticals and food, IoT-enabled sensors can monitor temperature and humidity levels during transportation. SAP S/4HANA can alert users to potential breaches in product quality and trigger actions to prevent spoilage or waste.

19.3.2 Predictive Maintenance with IoT Data

The combination of IoT and SAP S/4HANA is transforming maintenance operations by providing real-time data on equipment performance and enabling **predictive maintenance**. IoT sensors embedded in machinery can capture data on temperature, pressure, and vibration, allowing SAP S/4HANA to predict when equipment is likely to fail and schedule maintenance before a breakdown occurs.

This approach minimizes unplanned downtime, reduces maintenance costs, and extends the life of assets by ensuring that maintenance is performed only when necessary.

### 19.3.3 IoT-Driven Product Innovation

IoT enables businesses to collect data from their products after they have been sold and deployed in the field. This data can be analyzed in SAP S/4HANA to gain insights into product performance, customer usage patterns, and potential areas for improvement. By integrating IoT data with SAP S/4HANA's product lifecycle management (PLM) capabilities, businesses can accelerate product innovation, enhance customer satisfaction, and create new revenue streams through predictive maintenance and after-sales services.

## 19.4 Blockchain and SAP S/4HANA

**Blockchain** is an emerging technology that provides a decentralized and secure way to record transactions across multiple participants. SAP S/4HANA is exploring the use of blockchain to enhance transparency, traceability, and trust in supply chains, financial transactions, and contract management.

### 19.4.1 Supply Chain Traceability with Blockchain

Blockchain can be integrated into SAP S/4HANA to create a tamper-proof, transparent record of every transaction in a supply chain. This capability is particularly valuable in industries where traceability is critical, such as pharmaceuticals, agriculture, and manufacturing.

Key use cases of blockchain in supply chains include:

- **Product Provenance**: Blockchain can provide an immutable record of a product's journey from raw materials to the finished product, enabling businesses to trace the origin and authenticity of goods. This is especially important for industries that require compliance with regulations, such as food safety or pharmaceutical quality standards.
- **Supplier Verification**: Blockchain can enhance trust between supply chain partners by verifying supplier credentials and ensuring that products meet specified quality standards. It creates a transparent system where all parties can access the same transaction history.

19.4.2 Smart Contracts and Blockchain

**Smart contracts** are self-executing contracts with terms written directly into code. These contracts can be automatically enforced using blockchain technology. By integrating smart contracts with SAP S/4HANA, businesses can automate complex transactions such as procurement, payments, and contract management.

For example, a smart contract in SAP S/4HANA could automatically release payment to a supplier once goods are delivered and verified by IoT sensors, reducing the need for manual intervention and ensuring compliance with contract terms.

## 19.5 Cloud Adoption and SAP S/4HANA Cloud

As businesses continue to embrace cloud computing, **SAP S/4HANA Cloud** is becoming a critical component of many organizations' IT strategies. Cloud-based ERP systems offer several advantages, including lower upfront costs, faster deployment, and the ability to scale quickly. SAP S/4HANA Cloud is designed to support the needs of modern businesses by offering flexibility, agility, and innovation.

### 19.5.1 Rise of Hybrid and Multi-Cloud Strategies

One of the key trends in the adoption of SAP S/4HANA is the rise of **hybrid and multi-cloud strategies**. Businesses are increasingly adopting hybrid models that combine on-premise and cloud environments to gain the benefits of both. SAP S/4HANA Cloud provides the flexibility to run certain processes in the cloud while keeping sensitive data and custom applications on-premise.

**Multi-cloud strategies** allow businesses to choose multiple cloud service providers (e.g., AWS, Microsoft

Azure, Google Cloud) for different aspects of their operations. This flexibility enables organizations to optimize their cloud environments for cost, performance, and security.

19.5.2 SAP S/4HANA Cloud as a Platform for Innovation

SAP S/4HANA Cloud is not just an ERP system; it is also a platform for innovation. The cloud environment allows businesses to rapidly deploy new solutions, integrate with third-party services, and experiment with emerging technologies such as AI, ML, and IoT. SAP S/4HANA Cloud's integration with **SAP Business Technology Platform (BTP)** further enhances its ability to drive innovation by offering services for application development, data analytics, and AI.

### 19.6 The Role of Sustainability in SAP S/4HANA

Sustainability is becoming a major priority for businesses worldwide, and SAP S/4HANA is evolving to support organizations in achieving their environmental, social, and governance (ESG) goals. SAP S/4HANA provides tools for tracking and reporting sustainability metrics, optimizing resource use, and ensuring compliance with environmental regulations.

19.6.1 Carbon Footprint Tracking

SAP S/4HANA includes features that help businesses track their carbon footprint across operations. By analyzing energy consumption, raw material usage, and emissions data, businesses can identify opportunities to reduce their environmental impact. These insights can be integrated into the supply chain, production, and logistics processes to support sustainability initiatives.

19.6.2 Sustainable Supply Chain Management

Sustainability extends to supply chains, where SAP S/4HANA helps businesses optimize resource use, minimize waste, and ensure ethical sourcing practices. For example, businesses can track the sustainability credentials of suppliers, ensuring that products are sourced responsibly and meet regulatory standards.

SAP S/4HANA's integration with blockchain also enables greater transparency and traceability in the supply chain, helping businesses demonstrate compliance with sustainability goals and ensuring that products meet environmental standards.

## 19.7 Enhanced User Experience with SAP Fiori and AI-Powered Interfaces

The future of SAP S/4HANA will also focus on enhancing the user experience through the use of **SAP Fiori** and AI-powered interfaces. SAP is committed to making business applications more intuitive, user-friendly, and accessible across devices.

### 19.7.1 Voice-Activated Interfaces

Voice-activated interfaces are becoming more prevalent in business applications, and SAP S/4HANA is exploring the integration of **voice assistants** and **natural language processing (NLP)** to simplify user interactions. By allowing users to interact with the system using voice commands, SAP S/4HANA can streamline workflows and improve productivity, especially for tasks like data entry, report generation, and process approvals.

### 19.7.2 AI-Powered User Assistance

AI-powered user assistance, such as chatbots and virtual assistants, will continue to evolve within SAP S/4HANA. These tools help guide users through complex processes, provide instant answers to queries, and offer personalized recommendations based on user behavior. By integrating AI into the user interface, SAP S/4HANA can reduce the learning curve for new users and enhance overall efficiency.

## 19.8 Conclusion: The Future of SAP S/4HANA

The future of SAP S/4HANA is shaped by technological advancements such as AI, machine learning, IoT, blockchain, and cloud computing. These innovations are transforming the way businesses operate, offering new ways to automate processes, gain real-time insights, and enhance decision-making. As businesses adopt digital transformation strategies, SAP S/4HANA will continue to evolve, providing the tools needed to stay competitive in an increasingly complex and dynamic market.

In this chapter, we explored key trends such as AI and ML, IoT integration, blockchain applications, cloud adoption, sustainability, and the evolution of the user experience. By staying ahead of these trends, businesses can fully leverage SAP S/4HANA to drive innovation, efficiency, and long-term success.

In the next chapter, we will dive into **Case Studies and Success Stories in SAP S/4HANA**.

# Chapter 20: Case Studies and Success Stories in SAP S/4HANA

### 20.1 Introduction to SAP S/4HANA Case Studies

SAP S/4HANA has been adopted by thousands of businesses across various industries to transform their operations, drive digital transformation, and create new value. These companies have used SAP S/4HANA to streamline processes, enhance customer experiences, improve decision-making, and achieve significant cost savings. Each implementation offers unique insights into how businesses can leverage the full capabilities of SAP S/4HANA to meet their specific goals.

In this chapter, we will explore **real-world case studies** and **success stories** of companies that have implemented SAP S/4HANA. These examples span industries such as manufacturing, retail, finance, and healthcare, illustrating how organizations can overcome challenges, realize value, and gain a competitive edge using SAP S/4HANA.

### 20.2 Manufacturing Industry: Siemens Drives Efficiency with SAP S/4HANA

**Company**: Siemens
**Industry**: Manufacturing
**Solution**: SAP S/4HANA On-Premise

**Background**: Siemens, a global leader in manufacturing and engineering, needed a powerful, scalable ERP solution to manage its complex global supply chain and production processes. With operations in over 200 countries and a diverse product portfolio, Siemens required a solution that could support real-time data analysis, streamline workflows, and improve decision-making across its global operations.

**Challenges**:

- Fragmented legacy systems that limited real-time visibility into production and inventory.
- The need to streamline production planning, improve resource allocation, and enhance supply chain coordination.
- Difficulty in managing compliance with various industry standards and regulations across global operations.

**Solution**: Siemens implemented **SAP S/4HANA On-Premise** to replace its outdated systems and unify its core business processes. The system integrated with Siemens' existing technologies, such as **IoT** and **predictive analytics**, allowing the company to monitor and optimize production processes in real time. By leveraging **SAP Fiori** for user interfaces, Siemens enabled its employees to access personalized dashboards with real-time production data.

**Key Benefits**:

- **Real-Time Supply Chain Visibility**: Siemens gained full visibility into its global supply chain, enabling better resource allocation, demand forecasting, and inventory management.
- **Enhanced Production Efficiency**: By leveraging SAP S/4HANA's advanced analytics and IoT integration, Siemens improved production planning and reduced downtime by predicting machine failures and scheduling preventive maintenance.
- **Improved Compliance**: SAP S/4HANA enabled Siemens to automate regulatory compliance processes across different markets, ensuring adherence to local and global industry standards.

**Results**:

- Siemens achieved a **15% reduction in production lead times** through optimized planning and resource allocation.
- The company saw a **10% increase in asset uptime** due to predictive maintenance enabled by IoT integration.
- Real-time insights into inventory levels resulted in a **20% reduction in excess inventory**, improving cash flow and reducing storage costs.

### 20.3 Retail Industry: Under Armour Achieves Agility with SAP S/4HANA Cloud

**Company**: Under Armour
**Industry**: Retail
**Solution**: SAP S/4HANA Cloud

**Background**: Under Armour, a leading global sports apparel brand, sought to transform its retail operations to support rapid growth and the shift to digital commerce. The company required a cloud-based ERP system to manage its expanding global presence, improve operational efficiency, and create a more personalized customer experience.

**Challenges**:

- Managing a complex global supply chain while maintaining inventory accuracy across physical stores and online channels.
- The need for a flexible, scalable system that could support rapid expansion into new markets and channels.
- Legacy systems that hindered the company's ability to innovate and respond to changing consumer demands in real time.

**Solution**: Under Armour adopted **SAP S/4HANA Cloud** to standardize its global operations and drive greater agility in its retail processes. The cloud deployment allowed the company to scale its operations quickly while leveraging SAP S/4HANA's embedded analytics to gain real-time insights into customer behavior and sales trends.

**Key Benefits**:

- **Omnichannel Integration**: SAP S/4HANA Cloud enabled Under Armour to integrate its online and physical stores, providing a seamless customer experience across channels.
- **Personalized Customer Experiences**: By leveraging real-time data and customer insights, Under Armour personalized product recommendations, promotions, and marketing campaigns, driving higher customer engagement and loyalty.
- **Scalability for Global Expansion**: The cloud-based solution allowed Under Armour to quickly enter new markets and add new retail locations without the need for extensive infrastructure investments.

**Results**:

- Under Armour achieved a **25% increase in online sales** by integrating digital and physical retail channels and enhancing the customer experience.

- The company reduced inventory shortages by **30%**, improving product availability across global stores.
- With real-time analytics, Under Armour optimized its marketing campaigns, resulting in a **15% increase in conversion rates** across e-commerce platforms.

## 20.4 Financial Services Industry: Standard Chartered Bank Streamlines Operations with SAP S/4HANA

**Company**: Standard Chartered Bank
**Industry**: Financial Services
**Solution**: SAP S/4HANA Finance

**Background**: Standard Chartered Bank, a multinational banking and financial services company, needed a modern ERP system to streamline its financial operations, improve regulatory compliance, and enhance its ability to deliver new financial products. The bank sought to transform its financial processes to support real-time decision-making and increase transparency in its global operations.

**Challenges**:

- Legacy financial systems that were siloed and lacked real-time reporting capabilities.

- Increasing regulatory requirements across multiple regions, requiring a more transparent and auditable financial system.
- The need to deliver innovative financial services and products faster in a highly competitive market.

**Solution**: Standard Chartered Bank implemented **SAP S/4HANA Finance** to centralize its financial operations, improve reporting accuracy, and enhance compliance. The solution provided real-time financial data across all business units, enabling the bank to make faster, data-driven decisions.

**Key Benefits**:

- **Real-Time Financial Reporting**: SAP S/4HANA Finance provided the bank with real-time insights into financial performance, enabling more accurate and timely decision-making.
- **Enhanced Compliance**: The system automated compliance reporting, reducing the time and effort required to meet regulatory requirements across different jurisdictions.
- **Streamlined Operations**: By integrating all financial processes into a single platform, Standard Chartered Bank eliminated redundancies and reduced the time spent on manual reconciliation and reporting.

**Results**:

- The bank reduced its financial closing time by **40%**, enabling faster reporting and decision-making.
- Standard Chartered achieved a **30% reduction in compliance reporting costs** due to automation and enhanced transparency.
- The bank improved its overall operational efficiency, leading to **20% faster product development cycles** for new financial services.

**20.5 Healthcare Industry: Roche Enhances Patient Care with SAP S/4HANA and SAP Fiori**

**Company**: Roche
**Industry**: Healthcare and Pharmaceuticals
**Solution**: SAP S/4HANA On-Premise with SAP Fiori

**Background**: Roche, a global healthcare leader in pharmaceuticals and diagnostics, needed to improve its operational efficiency while ensuring the highest levels of regulatory compliance in its manufacturing and distribution processes. The company required an ERP system that could support real-time data visibility, enhance supply chain management, and streamline clinical trial processes to bring new drugs to market faster.

**Challenges**:

- Complex regulatory requirements across multiple countries and regions, requiring meticulous tracking and reporting of pharmaceutical manufacturing and distribution.
- Fragmented legacy systems that limited data visibility across production facilities and distribution centers.
- The need to accelerate clinical trials and bring new drugs to market more efficiently.

**Solution**: Roche implemented **SAP S/4HANA On-Premise** with **SAP Fiori** to centralize its operations and provide real-time insights into its manufacturing, supply chain, and clinical trial processes. The system's ability to automate compliance and provide advanced analytics helped Roche optimize production and improve patient outcomes.

**Key Benefits**:

- **Improved Supply Chain Management**: Roche gained full visibility into its global supply chain, enabling it to optimize inventory levels, reduce waste, and ensure timely distribution of pharmaceuticals.
- **Regulatory Compliance Automation**: SAP S/4HANA automated compliance tracking and reporting, ensuring that Roche met strict

regulatory requirements across different markets.

- **Accelerated Clinical Trials**: By streamlining clinical trial management and providing real-time data insights, SAP S/4HANA helped Roche reduce the time to market for new drugs.

**Results**:

- Roche reduced its overall supply chain costs by **15%** due to better inventory management and logistics optimization.
- The company achieved **30% faster clinical trial approval processes**, enabling faster delivery of life-saving drugs to patients.
- Compliance reporting time was reduced by **40%**, improving Roche's ability to respond to regulatory audits and requirements.

### 20.6 Conclusion: Leveraging SAP S/4HANA for Success

The case studies in this chapter demonstrate how companies across various industries have successfully implemented SAP S/4HANA to drive efficiency, innovation, and growth. By adopting SAP S/4HANA, these organizations have achieved real-time insights, streamlined processes, and enhanced their ability to respond to market demands and regulatory challenges.

From manufacturing to healthcare, SAP S/4HANA's flexibility and scalability have enabled companies to optimize their operations, reduce costs, and deliver superior customer experiences. These success stories illustrate the transformative power of SAP S/4HANA and provide valuable insights into how businesses can leverage the platform to achieve their strategic goals.

www.ingramcontent.com/pod-product-compliance
Lightning Source LLC
LaVergne TN
LVHW081753050326
832903LV00027B/1926